A Spirituality for Doing Justice

A Spirituality for Doing Justice

Reflections for Congregation-Based Organizers

✧ ✧ ✧

Dennis A. Jacobsen

Fortress Press
Minneapolis

A SPIRITUALITY FOR DOING JUSTICE
Reflections for Congregation-Based Organizers

Copyright 2021 © Fortress Press, an imprint of 1517 Media. All rights reserved. Except for brief quotations in critical articles or reviews, no part of this book may be reproduced in any manner without prior written permission from the publisher. Email copyright@1517.media or write to Permissions, Fortress Press, PO Box 1209, Minneapolis, MN 55440-1209.

Unless otherwise cited, the Scripture quotations are from New Revised Standard Version Bible, copyright © 1989 National Council of the Churches of Christ in the United States of America. Used by permission. All rights reserved worldwide.

Some Scripture quotations are from New Revised Standard Version Bible: Catholic Edition, copyright © 1989, 1993 National Council of the Churches of Christ in the United States of America. Used by permission. All rights reserved worldwide.

All of the psalms and the Magnificat in "The Daily Office for Doing Justice" are reprinted from *Psalms Anew: In Inclusive Language* (now out of print) and are used with the gracious permission of the authors Maureen Leach, OSF, and Nancy Schreck, OSF.

Print ISBN: 978-1-5064-6436-7
eBook ISBN: 978-1-5064-6437-4

Cover Design: Marti Naughton
Cover Images: Dennis Jacobsen; "Golden Wall with Paint Surface Texture," © Jesada Wongsa, Dreamstime.com

Interior design and typesetting: PerfecType | Nashville, TN

All icons in this book are by the hand of Dennis Jacobsen.

*For Tameem,
Lynn, Nora, Reena, and Wajdi.
Who would I be without you?*

CONTENTS

Preface: For the Love of God ... ix

PREPARATION

1. Iconography and Justice ... 3
2. Prayer Hut ... 9
3. The Process ... 13

REFLECTION

4. Weariness: *Elijah in the Cave* ... 19
5. Refreshment: *Fount of Living Water* ... 25
6. Divine Feminine: *Sophia* ... 35
7. Holy Faces: *Acheiropoietos* ... 45
8. Angelic Power: *Archangel Michael* ... 53
9. God Is Greater: *St. Francis and the Sultan* ... 61
10. Inner Harmony: *St. George and the Dragon* ... 67
11. Radical Personalism: *Dorothy Day* ... 73
12. Final Hope: *Christ in Glory* ... 79

PRACTICE

A Daily Office for Doing Justice ... 87

Gallery of Icons ... 197

PREFACE
For the Love of God

For many years I have reflected on a critique of congregation-based organizing made by Gregory Galluzzo, then executive director of Gamaliel, one of the national organizing networks. We were at a hotel bar in St. Louis, drinking wine after a long day of workshops and plenary sessions of the Gamaliel international leadership assembly, a gathering of about five hundred organizers and leaders from across the country and several from Great Britain and South Africa. Greg, a former Jesuit priest, said to me, "I've been organizing for more than thirty years, and I'm convinced that organizing helps me to fulfill the second great commandment of Jesus, to love my neighbor as myself. But I'm not so sure whether organizing helps me with the first great commandment."

Does congregation-based community organizing in fact deepen my love of God in accord with the first great commandment of Jesus and of Jewish tradition? Or does it serve as a distraction from that love or, even worse, something that moves me away from love of God? To organize for justice in the public arena through engagement of power and self-interest or through agitation and occasional confrontation is not some spiritually neutral exercise. Organizing can bring out the "better angels of our nature." It can also release the demons.

I've never bought the claim of some liberal Christians that loving my neighbor as myself fulfills the first great commandment of Jesus—to love God with all my heart and with all my soul and with all my mind. The first commandment is the greatest. The second is like it but not the same. One of the reasons I have committed the past thirty-four years of my life to congregation-based organizing is because of its faith dimension. I have been deeply inspired, particularly by some of the Baptist preachers and laity I have come to know and admire as we have struggled together in the trenches of social justice. I have seen how others love God even as they love their neighbor as themselves.

But has congregation-based organizing really deepened my love of God? Or has it seduced my ego and lifted the lid off of my worst impulses? In so many ways, I understand why pastors prefer the safety of the sanctuary to the rough-and-tumble realm of organizing for justice. The sanctuary offers prayerful peacefulness and devotion to God. Particularly as I age, I have respect for those who faithfully enter the inner room of their soul to meet and love God. Social action is messy and disruptive and noisy. While actively serving Jesus, Martha was worried and distracted by many things. Mary chose the better part, the one thing that mattered.

I won't go into the biblical and theological reasons why I think congregation-based organizing offers a faithful way of living out the teachings of Jesus. I tried to do that in my first book, *Doing Justice: Congregations and Community Organizing*. What I am attempting to offer in this book is a kind of personal response to Greg's critique. I am seeking to integrate congregation-based community organizing with iconography. I am hinting at a spiritual foundation that, in my mind, is requisite for faithful organizing. Martha and Mary, I think, are mirror images of each other. Both need each other to create something whole and life-giving and faithful to the two great commandments of Jesus.

Over the past decades, my engagement in peace and justice struggles has been an anvil of the soul where my faith has been forged, shaped, and tested. I have tried, in my own stumbling way, to live out the first two great commandments of Jesus and to integrate them into the center of my being. And so I write from the heat of experience and not as a cool observer. I have been blessed with so many rich experiences and been deepened by hundreds of leaders, organizers, and activists. I have been engaged in congregation-based organizing since 1985, when I was a cofounder of an Industrial Areas Foundation (IAF) organization in Jersey City. That was also the year I began studying iconography under the master iconographer Vladislav Andrejev at the School of Sacred Arts in Manhattan. I was a founding pastor of Milwaukee Inner-city Congregations Allied for Hope (MICAH) and served for almost twenty years as director of the Gamaliel National Clergy Caucus. For many years I led the Congregation-Based Organizing Team of the Evangelical Lutheran Church in America and helped to form the Interfaith Organizing Initiative. I continue to be a leader in MICAH.

The first thing the reader might notice about this book is that it is short. I attribute the book's brevity to the searing truths of two fortune cookies that I opened on two consecutive dining occasions at two different Chinese restaurants in Manhattan. The first told me that I have "some talent but little ambition." The second, which

PREFACE

Lynn (my spouse) has threatened to put on my tombstone as an epitaph, told me that I am a "jack of all trades, master of none." The truth hurts. I'm neither sufficiently talented nor ambitious enough to write a magnum opus. After four decades of rather intense engagement in congregation-based organizing and some on-again, off-again efforts at painting icons, I think I do have something to say as a journeyman jack of all trades. The reader will decide whether the book should have been longer or even shorter.

The second half of this book is called a "Daily Office for Doing Justice," which has its own introduction. My hope is that the reader will give this a try for four weeks, entering the daily rhythm of brief morning and evening readings, prayer, and reflection.

As I write these words, my daughter Nora is in her eighth month of pregnancy with my first grandchild. I pray for Tameem every day and think of what an incredible gift he is to me and will be to the world. I'm seventy-one years old. I may live until he becomes a young adult, or the divine hook may yank me off life's stage long before then. I'd like Tameem to know something about what his grandfather believed and how he tried to live. So, Tameem, although this book is certainly dedicated to your mom, Nora; your dad, Wajdi; your aunt Reena; and your grandmother Lynn, it is especially dedicated to you.

Preparation

CHAPTER 1
Iconography and Justice

My journey into iconography began in 1985 when I enrolled in a class taught by the master iconographer Vladislav Andrejev at the (now defunct) School of Sacred Arts in Manhattan. At the time I was the pastor of Trinity Lutheran Church, an African American congregation in a tough part of Jersey City. Along with other religious leaders, I was developing a congregation-based organization in Jersey City affiliated with the Industrial Areas Foundation (IAF). I was active in the Kairos community, a group of Christians organizing nonviolent civil disobedience actions against nuclear weapons. Kairos was small in size but remarkable in giftedness, including in its ranks Fr. Daniel Berrigan, Sr. Anne Montgomery, Elmer Maas, Fr. Ned Murphy, Fr. Jack Egan, Rev. John Backe, and other notable peace activists. In short, I was engaged in urban ministry, congregation-based organizing for social justice, and direct action against nuclear weapons at the same time that I was studying to become an iconographer. I viewed iconography as integral to my efforts as an urban pastor, peacemaker, and social justice organizer. Iconography was not merely an aesthetic escape or an emotional relief. Rather, it deepened and centered me spiritually, helped me to become more whole as a person engaged in public life, quieted my ego, and integrated my faith and my actions.

Icons do not invite one into a separate, transcendent reality removed from the anguish and joy of earthly existence. The theology of icons is rooted in the incarnation of God in Christ Jesus. Icons portray the infusion of the divine into the mundane. I think here of the Lutheran conception of the Eucharist as consubstantiation: the body and blood of Christ is present in, with, and under the bread and the wine of holy communion. There is a kind of concentration of awareness here. If I can see Christ present in bread and wine, perhaps I can begin to see Christ present within me; within the person next to me at the communion rail; and within the hungry, the sick, the naked, the thirsty, the imprisoned, and the immigrant stranger. Perhaps I can even begin to see Christ present within all of human history and all of creation. I long to see as Mechtild of Magdeburg (thirteenth century) saw: "The day of my spiritual awakening was the day I saw and knew I saw all things in God and God in all things."[1] I am moved by the encompassing vision of Hildegard of Bingen (twelfth century): "Just as a circle embraces all that is within it, so does the God-head embrace all. No one has the power to divide this circle, to surpass it, or to limit it."[2]

All reality is infused with the presence of God. Icons invite us into this mystery through a concentration of our awareness on Christ,

---

1. Matthew Fox, *Christian Mystics, 365 Readings and Meditations* (Novato, CA: New World Library, 2011). For the original work, see Mechtild of Magdeburg, *The Flowing Light of God*, trans. Frank Tobin (Mahwah, NJ: Paulist Press, 1998).
2. Hildegard of Bingen, *Scivias* (1151), quoted in Renate Craine, *Hildegard, Prophet of the Cosmic Christ* (New York: Crossroad Publishing, 1997).

the incarnation of God, or on a saint portrayed in the icon whose life was filled with the divine. In my own stumbling way, I try to deepen my engagement in social justice through iconography. God is present in the agony of human suffering and in the beauty of human struggle, but it is easy to become spiritually lost in that suffering and struggle. Icons gently guide us toward a vision of God who is within all and beyond all, who is present in the suffering and in the struggle, and who embraces all reality with divine love.

Traditional iconography uses only natural materials: wood board, rabbit skin or fish glue, crushed marble gesso, red clay, ground pigments, egg tempera, gold leaf, linseed oil. The icon uses the animal, mineral, and vegetable world to glorify God. The substance of material reality praises God through the icon and invites the icon viewer to see the presence of God in the substance of material reality. Icons express in visual form what Gerard Manley Hopkins expressed in his poem "God's Grandeur": "The world is charged with the grandeur of God."[3]

A cautionary word for my activism: "When people are too weak for contemplation, they switch to action, which is a mere shadow of contemplation and of reason. Since, owing to the weakness of their souls, their faculty of contemplation is insufficient, they cannot grasp the object of their contemplation and be fulfilled by it. Yet they still want to see it, and so they switch to action, in order

---

3. Gerard Manley Hopkins, *Poems of Gerard Manley Hopkins*, ed. Robert Bridges (London: Humphrey Milford, 1918). Originally written in 1877.

to see with their eyes what they could not see with their spirit" (Plotinus, Enneads III 8.4. 33–39).[4]

Rabbi Abraham Joshua Heschel, who marched with Rev. Martin Luther King Jr. across the Pettus Bridge from Selma to Montgomery a few days after the police brutality of Bloody Sunday, said, "The road to the sacred leads through the secular."[5] I know this to be true. I abhor any notion of the sacred that hides from the secular or despises it. I know that if I imagine that I will find God by fleeing a suffering world, the only god I will find will be the god of my imagination. I do not leave the sacred when I leave the icon board and enter the secular world of compromise, politics, negotiations, and power. In all the messiness of the world, God is to be found. I do not worship a deus ex machina, a god who sets the world in motion or shows up occasionally to fix things and then retreats. I worship the God who is present in all creation and in all of human history. Iconography offers me renewal, clarity, liminality, and integrated spirituality—but not escape. Rabbi Heschel reminds me: "Worship is a way of seeing the world in the light of God."[6] So is iconography.

A Lutheran perspective on iconography sustains a focus on grace and on the *simul iustus et peccator* reality of my existence. If I waited to be holy enough to deserve to create an icon, the board would remain blank. I approach the board painfully aware not only of my

---

4. Pierre Hadot, *Plotinuus or the Simplicity of Vision* (Chicago: University of Chicago Press, 1998), 43.
5. Abraham Heschel, *Between God and Man* (New York: Simon and Schuster, 1997), 147.
6. Abraham Heschel, *I Asked for Wonder* (New York: Crossroad, 1983), 20.

considerable technical constraints but also of my deep spiritual limitations. The process of iconography aids me in my sanctification, not the other way around.

The danger of iconography is that it is vulnerable to becoming religious. I mean *religious* in the way that Dietrich Bonhoeffer used this term when he wrote from Tegel prison: "The 'religious act' is always something partial; 'faith' is something whole, involving the whole of one's life."[7] Religion keeps us in the sanctuary. Faith propels us into the public arena. Religion is privatistic. Faith is always communal. Religion proclaims justice only in terms of personal righteousness. Faith struggles for justice in the public realm. Religion spiritualizes the spiritual. Faith embodies the spiritual. Religion announces peace when there is no peace. Faith seeks peace through justice. Religion says *yes* to prosperity but *no* to justice; *yes* to health but *no* to the cross; *yes* to a personal relationship with Jesus but *no* to the prophetic claim of Christ on my life; *yes* to an end to suffering in the next life but *no* to confrontation with the principalities and powers that inflict warfare and poverty on God's children now. Religion is always more popular than faith, but it is also a profanation of the gospel. I pray that my iconography is an expression of faith.

Relentless activism starves my soul and makes me hunger for the prayerful focus of iconography. Prayer and action feed each other and need each other in order to become something whole and meaningful. Dan Berrigan puts it this way: "There is a cult, an

---

7. Dietrich Bonhoeffer, *Letters and Papers from Prison*, ed. Eberhard Bethge (New York: MacMillan, 1967), 191.

idolatry of action. There is an idolatry, a cult of prayer. The first is a mad escape, the second a consumer item, a narcotic. . . . Each taken alone, activism, passivism, without the other, is hardly recognizable as a human activity; the activists grow sour, violence-prone; the meditators dwell on the moon, lunar. The question is not merely one of integrating these two. The question is how to recover each of these two, shapeless, defamed and lost: meaningless action, pointless prayer."[8]

Icons connect us with the immaterial realm of reality. Materialistic scientism allows for no such realm. That an immaterial realm of the divine, angels, and the faithful departed exists seems fanciful, imaginary, an illusory projection, a throwback to medieval cosmology. I can offer no convincing reason why I believe in such a realm. I resonate with Blaise Pascal: "The heart has its reasons of which reason knows nothing."[9] I believe in an immaterial realm that is more real than material reality—to the bemusement of my agnostic, secular humanist, and atheistic friends. Even as I believe that God is panentheistic spirit, so I believe that there is a spiritual realm that interacts continuously with the material reality in which I live. I am drawn to the ancient Celtic notion of "thin places"—liminal spaces where there is a thin membrane between the material and spiritual realms. Icons draw me into liminality, connecting my material existence with the immaterial realm, revealing to me the active presence of God in human anguish, human struggle, and human achievement.

---

8. *Peacemaking: Day by Day* (Pax Christi USA, 1985), May 19.
9. From *Pensées*, 443, and quoted in James M. Byrne, *Religion and the Enlightenment: From Descartes to Kant* (Louisville, KY: Westminster John Knox, 1996), 87.

Prayer Hut (Gallery A)

CHAPTER 2
Prayer Hut

In my uneven prayer life, I seek wholeness and awareness of the presence of God. I attempt a spiritual discipline that connects iconography with my personal journey and with the struggle for justice.

The prayer hut in the backyard beckons my soul. Come and rest. Come and find solace. Come and seek wisdom. Come and be centered. Sit. Light a votive candle and an incense stick. Breathe in the silence. Pray. Chant a psalm. Read Scripture. Gaze within. Remember. Who do you claim to be? Who have you been? Who does God will you to be?

Look at what is placed in this small, sacred space:

- the icons, damaged by exposure to harsh Wisconsin winters even as we humans are worn and world-wearied by exposure to harsh realities;
- the stained-glass cross from Lynn—she fills your life with loving light;
- the fossil that Nora gave you when you had your father-daughter time in Arizona just before she married Wajdi;
- the hazelnut that reminds you of Reena and her award-winning essay on Julian of Norwich: "And in this vision he

showed me a little thing, the size of a hazel-nut, lying in the palm of my hand, and to my mind's eye it was round as any ball. I looked at it and thought, 'What can this be?' And the answer came to me, 'It is all that is made.' I wondered how it could last, for it was so small I thought it might suddenly disappear. And the answer in my mind was, 'It lasts and will last forever because God loves it; and in the same way everything exists through the love of God'";[1]

- the turquoise and silver pill case that your father used for his meds before that horrible, suicidal hospice death;
- the fossil from Germany that Dan Berrigan, poet-prophet-mentor-friend, gave you as a birthday gift: "May you live as long as God does!";
- the rosary that Ana Garcia Ashley, director of Gamaliel, generously and publicly presented to you—the rosary that she prayerfully carried when arrested at the White House on behalf of undocumented immigrants;
- the glass container of colored sand—a mixture of various sands from Gamaliel affiliate organizations around the country, blessed in worship at a Gamaliel national leadership assembly;
- the scarf gently placed over your head at the funeral service for six Sikhs massacred in their temple by a white supremacist;
- the pill vial filled with soil from the grounds of Incarnation and with a Bible passage—an invitation to the Holy Ground tent revival. (Remember how someone was shot

---

1. Julian of Norwich, *Revelations of Divine Love*, trans. Elizabeth Spearing (London: Penguin Books, 1998), 7.

five times in the chest just minutes before the service started and how the police sealed off the street in front of the church with yellow tape. Holy Ground, indeed!).

The prayer hut weaves together central relationships of your life, organizing efforts, struggles amid injustice, urban parish ministry, and iconography. How blessed you are. Sit. Be still. Remember. Your life is woven by Sophia, the Holy Spirit of God.

Weaver of worlds, seen and unseen, weaver of light and darkness, weal and woe, and weaver of the warp and weft of history, weave my life into the fabric of your will.

Try now, in your own fumbling way, to weave together the icons and the organizing.

CHAPTER 3
The Process

After a period of prayerful reflection, research, and painfully slow drawing of the icon pattern (when I am creating my own), I pray for God's forgiveness, guidance, and grace, and then I start working on the icon. The icon uses only natural materials. I start with a rough board of basswood, which I cut with a handsaw into the dimensions I want. Then I shape the inner frame with a router (sometimes I prefer not to have an inner frame) and sand the wood. I have little skill in woodworking, but I like the rough-hewn effect. After an application of rabbit skin glue, I apply eight to ten layers of gesso with intermittent sanding and a final fine sanding to attain a smooth marble finish. The laborious preparation is complete and forms both the material and spiritual foundation of the icon. Recall the words of Jesus: "On this rock I will build my church" (Matt 16:18).

Skilled iconographers etch the pattern of the icon into the gesso. I use carbon paper and a hard pencil. The layers of paint are applied with egg tempera and ground pigments. In canonical iconography, the movement from dark to light color in the application of several layers of egg tempera symbolizes spiritual transformation. For example, the original color of the face and hands is *sankir*, a mixture of olive green, deep ochre, and burnt sienna. This resultant muddy green color is followed by two series of highlights and floatings, using white mixed with cadmium orange, flame red, mars yellow, or red ochre. The final touch is painting the direction of the eyes by applying pure white beneath and on an edge of each eye. The movement is from dark colors to light, from spiritual darkness to illuminating light.

This symbolism is particularly strong in the halo, which begins with three layers of red clay sanded to a mirror finish and burnished with an agate. The red clay symbolizes Adam, whose name in Hebrew means "ground" or "clay." Vodka is then applied to a small section of the halo. As the vodka dries, I exhale deeply onto the halo and then quickly apply gold leaf. A chemical bonding occurs. Gold represents the divine principle. Just as God breathed life into Adam, so the breath of the iconographer symbolizes the very beginning of the union of the earthly clay with the divine element of gold. The transition from red clay to gold symbolizes the transfiguration desired by God, made possible by Christ, and effected by the activity of the Holy Spirit. As the apostle Paul says, "And all of us, with unveiled faces, seeing the glory of the Lord as though reflected in a mirror, are being transformed into the same image from one degree of glory to another; for this comes from the Lord, the Spirit" (2 Cor 3:18). The Greek word for "image" here is *icon*. God intends for us to be living icons. The Orthodox tradition is bold about this spiritual transformation: "The rebirth of man consists in changing 'the present humiliated state' of his nature, making it participate in the divine life, because, according to the classical phrase of St. Gregory the Theologian, who echoes St. Basil the Great, 'Man is a creature, but he is commanded to become God.'"[1]

---

1. Leonid Ouspensky, *Theology of the Icon, Volume 1*, trans. Anthony Gythiel (Crestwood, NY: St. Vladimir's Seminary Press, 1992), 158.

Fortunately for me, a Lutheran iconographer who sees little evidence of my own spiritual transformation, all is not light and gold in the icon. There remains red clay, unburnished, on the sides of the frame—a reminder of the persistence of the old Adam. In Lutheran language, we remain *simul iustus et peccator*—saint and sinner at the same time.

When the work on the icon is completed, I offer a prayer of blessing with incense and apply a heated mixture of linseed oil and stand oil. Materials from the animal, mineral, and vegetable world are thus bound together and used to glorify God who creates all, sustains all, and invites all into the divine presence.

The glorification of God through the spiritual energy, symbolism, and natural materials of the icon can be understood from a Lutheran perspective as a strong example of the Lutheran theological principle of *finitum capax infiniti*. The finite is capable of the infinite. God is present everywhere at once in the cosmos and yet is not delimited by the cosmos. God is both transcendent and immanent, whose essence is unknowable and who is incarnate in the human being Jesus. Christ is present in the Eucharist. The church is the body of Christ. The icon invites us to open our eyes to see the presence of God in all of creation. If we can see something holy, something Christlike, in an icon, perhaps we can see a little more clearly the presence of the incarnate Christ in each human being, particularly those within whom Christ promised to be present: the one who is hungry, who is thirsty, who is a stranger, who is naked, who is sick, who is in prison.

Reflection

Elijah in the Cave (Gallery B)
11"x14" wood panel.
Egg tempera and gold leaf.

CHAPTER 4
Weariness:
Elijah in the Cave

The story of Elijah in the cave on Mount Horeb (1 Kings 19), hiding from his enemies and feeling utterly alone, speaks directly to the experience of many of us. I painted this icon (see gallery B) while on sabbatical, emotionally and spiritually exhausted, wondering whether my efforts in community organizing and in parish ministry were making any difference at all. In most versions of this icon, Elijah holds the scroll of a prophet. I chose to omit the scroll. I wanted to depict the prophet as being bereft even of the word of God. The icon shows Elijah sustained, quite simply, by a raven rather than an angel. The dark night of the soul may need to be endured before experiencing the presence of God, who appears to Elijah neither in a great wind nor in an earthquake or fire, but in a gentle, challenging whisper: "What are you doing here, Elijah?"

On my sabbatical, I felt the need to go deeper spiritually, even if that meant entering a place of inner darkness. I needed to confront my sense of discouragement and to find some spiritual reservoir to sustain me in ministry and organizing. In short, I needed to experience my own kind of Elijah cave. Privileged to have received a Lilly Foundation grant, I traveled to Crete and found my way to Zoures Cave, the fourteenth-century dwelling place of the legendary Ninety-Eight Holy Fathers. I drove the short distance from Paleochora to Azogires. With no ability to speak Greek, I was unable to get any directions to the cave. I tried a few roads, but the effort was futile. Just when I was about to give up, I saw a sign directing me to the cave. I parked where the road stopped and walked up a rocky path for about twenty minutes to the cave entrance.

I could see why many people turn back at this point. The cave entrance is foreboding. The descent is into dank darkness. I had a small flashlight, which showed me a broken iron-rung ladder leading down into the cave. My rational side was very clear: this is too risky. This place is desolate, and I am alone. What if I break my ankle? What if the flashlight goes out? But I had come this far and didn't want my fears to block me from entering into a cave where saints had somehow lived and prayed together seven hundred years ago. I climbed down into the darkness. The last rung of the ladder was several feet from the cave floor. I jumped—a kind of leap of faith into darkness and uncertainty, which is what I surely needed spiritually. If I was going to go deeper within myself, perhaps I needed to enter, albeit ever so briefly, a place where holy fathers had lived communally and fearlessly so long ago. I can't articulate the profound nature of this experience for me. Entering darkness may require a solitary journey, but it can also become a way of encountering the holiness, courage, trust, prayerfulness, and remarkable faith of the ancient ones. Perhaps it may even be a way of hearing a whispered word from God.

I explored the first level of the cave and found a small table on which an icon of the holy fathers rested. I walked farther into the cave and saw another precipitous descent into darkness and heard the sound of water. At this point my rational side took over. I turned back and climbed back up into warmth and sunlight.

When I returned to Milwaukee, I began to paint this *Elijah in the Cave* icon.

✧ ✧ ✧

An Elijah cave can be as simple as a kitchen table. Delores Haslem was one of the saintly members of Incarnation Lutheran Church in Milwaukee, where I served as pastor for twenty-six years. Delores arose at four o'clock every morning and spent an hour sitting at her kitchen table, reading her Bible and praying. Having endured much suffering in her life and always giving generously of herself, she was sustained and guided by her solitary prayer life. I don't think we can reach spiritual depth without entering into spiritual discipline. Each of us is different, so a profound spiritual discipline for one may be an empty experience for another. Part of the journey into the cave is discovering a discipline that can sustain us in darkness and discouragement. On and off, I paint icons, sit in my prayer hut, and internalize the Jesus Prayer ("Lord Jesus Christ, Son of God, have mercy on me, a sinner").[1]

I would benefit greatly from a bit more discipline.

✧ ✧ ✧

When I told Gregory Galluzzo, founding director of Gamaliel, that I was writing this book, he remarked on the importance of having spiritual depth if one is doing organizing work: "If you are not spiritually centered, you can't stay in the center of the storm." Greg recalled organizers in recovery who succumbed to their drug

---

1. Widely used especially in the Orthodox Church, the Jesus Prayer can be traced back to the sixth century. Diadochos taught that repetition of the prayer leads to inner stillness and is a precious way of living out St. Paul's urging in 1 Thessalonians 5:17 that we pray without ceasing.

addictions shortly after entering the organizing world. Spiritually untethered, they could not stay healthy amid the intense daily pressures of their profession.

Greg also shared with me an anecdote about his wife, Mary Gonzales, who is widely esteemed as one of the great congregation-based organizers in the country. Early in her career, Mary attended a national training event. One of the trainers, clearly a bit envious of Mary's skill and growing reputation, decided to bring her down a few notches in a session he was leading.

"How many one-on-ones have you done this week?" he challenged Mary.

"Twenty," Mary responded.

"Well, okay, but how much money have you raised by yourself so far this year?"

"One hundred fifty thousand dollars," said Mary.

Getting a bit desperate, the trainer tried a different tactic: "Fine, but when was your last public action?"

"Last Thursday," Mary answered.

Feeling agitated, the trainer blurted out: "But do you play the piano?"

"No," admitted Mary.

Triumphant, the trainer shouted, "Well, that's your problem!"

The story is an entertaining accounting of an agitation gone badly. But Greg also said that on one level, the trainer had a point. Activity, even remarkably skilled and successful activity, is insufficient for an organizer. A creative center, a spirituality for the long haul, is absolutely essential. Mary, by the way, may not play the piano, but she has such a center as well as remarkable spiritual depth.

✧ ✧ ✧

On occasion, I try to enter my inner cave not only to find a spiritual reservoir but also to confront the demons that lurk in my darkness. My demons may not equal those of some in the public arena, including certain politicians who will remain unnamed, but I've got quite a bit of my own shadow material to work on. The last thing the public arena needs is more unhinged personalities mixing things up and projecting their inner demons into the world around them.

I recall a letter I received from Elizabeth McAlister while she was in the District of Columbia jail for an act of civil disobedience. She was being threatened by violent cellmates. Liz wrote that they were "striking matches off their private hells." That metaphor has stayed with me. If we don't carefully tend to our souls, our actions may be fueled by our inner hells.

Conflating narratives in 1 Kings 17 and 1 Kings 19, the icon depicts a raven offering a morsel of bread to Elijah. It may not seem like much, but it is sufficient for the prophet's need. The fact is that God offers us bread for the journey, often from unusual sources and often in unpredictable ways. What person of faith has not had the experience of being unexpectedly fed precisely at the point where they were feeling spiritually empty and soul-starved?

My own essential sustenance is provided by the Eucharist. In my retirement, I am a member of Hephatha Lutheran Church in the 53206 zip code of Milwaukee, a geography of racialized, concentrated poverty and grim oppression. Under the guidance of its remarkably talented pastor, Rev. Mary Martha Kannass, the congregation organizes, serves, grieves, and celebrates. Each Sunday, Pastor Kannass selects different members of the laity to distribute the bread and wine of the Eucharist. I am especially grateful when I receive bread from the hand of someone who has endured their own experience of the dark cave: a prisoner on release for a few hours, an addict in recovery, a leader who has struggled for justice for decades with little to show for it: "Take and eat. The body of Christ, given for you."

I may enter the sanctuary feeling hungry, but I always leave feeling fed.

CHAPTER 5
Refreshment: *Fount of Living Water*

Fount of Living Water (Gallery C)
11"x14" wood panel.
Egg tempera and gold leaf.

> Those who drink of the water that I will give them will never be thirsty. The water that I will give will become in them a spring of water gushing up to eternal life. (John 4:14)

> Let anyone who is thirsty come to me, and let the one who believes in me drink. As the scripture has said, "Out of the believer's heart shall flow rivers of living water." (John 7:37–38)

> I am thirsty. (John 19:28)

On the aforementioned sabbatical, I had the great privilege of visiting the Church of St. Mary of Blachernae in Istanbul, which contains a *hagiasma*, a holy well, that draws water from a nearby spring reputed since pre-Christian times to have miraculous healing powers. This is a sacred site in the Orthodox Church and serves as inspiration for icons of the *Fount of Living Water*, better known as the Life-Giving Spring of the Mother of God. On the same sabbatical trip, I saw the splendid fifteenth-century version of this icon by Angelos Akotantos in the Hodegetria

Monastery on Crete. Moved both by the Blachernae hagiasma and the Angelos icon, I brought home a vial of water from the fount in the Church of St. Mary of Blachernae and used some of it to mix with pigments and egg tempera in the making of this *Fount of Living Water* icon. From Mary and the Christ child flow waters of salvation for both physical and spiritual healing.

Those who thirst for justice can get quite thirsty at times. Organizing, while often exhilarating, can also feel dry and stale. There is little satisfaction in issue campaigns that become protracted and end up failing or in victories that prove temporary and are overturned by the next mayor or governor. The political landscape can feel like a barren desert. I often have resonated with the words of the psalmist: "O God, you are my God, I seek you, my soul thirsts for you; my flesh faints for you, as in a dry and weary land where there is no water" (Ps 63:1).

What quenches my thirst? Is it just victory and adrenaline rush in the public arena? Or is my thirst satisfied by drawing on the life-giving waters of Christ to sustain me in the struggle? Perhaps satisfied—but surely not quenched. Even Jesus was thirsty on the cross.

The life-giving waters of Christ are profoundly experienced in baptism. Here the fount of the hagiasma is joined to the baptismal font, a life-giving spring that bubbles up in a simple basin of water. The gifts of baptism are breathtaking: rebirth, spiritual cleansing, spiritual renewal, "a spring of water gushing up to eternal life," life-giving water for life's desert places, a sealing by the Holy Spirit, marked by the cross of Christ forever, reclaimed as a precious child of God—a sacred reminder, a sacred remembering of one's identity, a sacred trust and responsibility of being welcomed into a community of faith that struggles for justice and peace on earth and is cheered on by the communion of saints in heaven.

The life-giving waters of baptism lead to the eschatological life-giving waters of the life to come: "They will hunger no more, and thirst no more; the sun will not strike them, nor any scorching heat; for the Lamb at the center of the throne will be their shepherd, and he will guide them to springs of the water of life, and God will wipe away every tear from their eyes" (Rev 7:16–17).

I wish baptism was a magic act. I wish it could instantly, visibly, unalterably transform everyone who is blessed with this life-giving water. As a parish pastor, I was deeply privileged to baptize many infants, children, teens, and a few adults. I felt joy in doing so. And later, sometimes, I felt sorrow.

I am still deeply troubled by the inability of the congregation—and of myself as pastor—to protect a young man from the evil that awaited him when he left the sanctuary of the baptismal font and returned to the streets. Benny was fourteen years old when I baptized him. I learned from a teacher that standardized testing placed him at genius level. He was a natural leader. He was also susceptible to the streets and was running with a gang. Benny became active in some of the youth ministries of the church. When our MICAH Holy Ground task force organized to improve the local park, Benny was key to our victory.

The splash pad at Lindbergh Park was nonfunctional due to deteriorated plumbing. The fieldhouse had no running water and was filled with mold. Broken glass was everywhere. The drinking fountains didn't work. The playground equipment was mostly broken. Gang activity made the park a scary place for children and elderly persons. At a MICAH public meeting, our county supervisor announced that he would seek a million dollars for renovation of Lindbergh Park in the preliminary county budget. He did so, but he received only mixed support from the other supervisors on the Milwaukee County parks committee. Our hopes hinged on the outcome of the county budget hearing. Several hundred people were present to advocate for their various causes. Several members of our Holy Ground task force spoke on behalf of renovation of Lindbergh Park. The county board of supervisors listened politely. But when fourteen-year-old Benny spoke, the room became quiet, and the supervisors became attentive. Benny was articulate and convincing. The result was unanimous approval of more than $1 million for the park's renovation, including a new splash pad—flowing fountains of water to refresh playful children in the heat of the summer.

At a tent revival on the church grounds that summer, Benny offered a testimony. He said that as a young African American male, the options for his future looked to be either going to prison or dying on the streets. But Benny said, "Because of the love of this church and of my parents, I have been saved from the belly of the beast." I felt like the life-giving waters of baptism were flowing forth from him.

The streets fought back and reclaimed him. Benny began to drift away from the church. He began to run his own gang and claimed Lindbergh Park as his turf. He was locked up for a few months. When Benny violated the conditions of his release, I learned that the police were looking for him. It was Holy Week. After the Good Friday noon service, I sensed that I should look for him too. I found Benny at Lindbergh Park. We went to the parish house to talk. I convinced Benny to turn himself in to avoid a dangerous confrontation with the police.

For the next several years, Benny drifted in and out of jail. I made unsuccessful attempts to reach him. His older brother, whom I visited in prison, let me know how Benny was doing. The worst news was hearing that Benny had been shot eight times by a rival. Somehow Benny survived, but he is now lame in one leg. The joy that I had felt in Benny's baptism turned to sorrow—sorrow upon sorrow because several other young people whom I had baptized have been shot to death. I wonder: How do the living waters of baptism contend with the effluent of the streets? How do we organize in ways that might truly save young people like Benny from the belly of the beast?

In Milwaukee, as in all too many cities, the water is hardly life-giving. The city does a good job of purifying the water that comes from Lake Michigan. The problem is an aging delivery system. More than seventy-two thousand homes get their water through service lines that are constructed of lead. This creates an unpredictable but all too real risk that water used for drinking or cooking will be contaminated with lead. To replace these lead pipes will cost about a billion dollars. At the current pace of replacement, it will take Milwaukee eighty-six years to have all its service lines lead-free. And that assumes that homeowners will pay for the costly replacement of the service line from the curb to the home, as the city accepts responsibility only for replacement from the water main to the curb. To complicate matters more, even where older buildings do not have a lead service line, interior sources of lead in plumbing, such as lead solder, can contribute significantly to lead poisoning at the tap.

Even low levels of lead exposure can cause permanent brain damage and negatively affect learning, behavior, and health throughout a child's life. Although lead poisoning is no respecter of persons, the poor are hit hardest. Medicaid-enrolled children in Wisconsin are at three times greater risk of lead poisoning than non-Medicaid-enrolled children. More than 30 percent of African American children in Milwaukee live in dire poverty. Almost 50 percent are income eligible for free school lunches. In 2016 African American children accounted for 50 percent of all lead-poisoned children in Wisconsin, even though they constituted only 21 percent of all children tested. Of 13,540 African American children tested that year, 1,791 (13.2%) were found to be lead poisoned. The rate of lead-poisoned children in the neighborhood of my home congregation, Hephatha Lutheran Church, is a terrifying 24 percent.[1]

The city focuses on lead abatement and the risks of poisoning from lead paint. Lead paint continues to be the primary cause of lead poisoning and merits intense efforts at remedy. But lead in water is also a grave concern. The EPA estimates that drinking water can make up 20 percent or more of a person's total exposure to lead. Infants who consume mostly mixed formula can receive 40–60 percent of their exposure to lead from drinking water. The city has done little to address this issue other than replacing lead service lines at a snail's pace or recommending that concerned residents purchase water filters for their homes or run their faucets for a few minutes before drinking. Some neighborhood organizations valiantly attempt to educate residents in low-income

---

1. Wisconsin Childhood Lead Poisoning Prevention Program, "2016 Report on Childhood Lead Poisoning in Wisconsin" (Madison, WI: Wisconsin Department of Health Services, 2017), 10, 13, 23.

neighborhoods and provide free water filters as their limited dollars allow.

How can churches baptize from a font of living water and not demand that the city ensure purity of water for all of God's children, whether baptized or not? When I first became aware of this issue through a lead-safe education event at Hephatha, I convened an exploratory meeting of interested persons. Within two months we decided to form the Coalition on Lead Emergency (COLE), which now consists of a dozen respected organizations. Given my experience in congregation-based organizing through Milwaukee Inner-City Congregations Allied for Hope (MICAH), I have a good idea of the steps that need to be taken to win essential policy reforms and what kind of pushback we will likely get. I am particularly encouraged that we are rapidly developing a strong base of residents directly affected by lead service lines.

COLE's first issue cut was envisioned by Pastor Mary Martha Kannass: providing every birthing mother in Milwaukee with a free lead-education kit prior to hospital discharge, including an NSF/ANSI Standard 53 certified lead filter water pitcher and two replacement filters. Each year about ten thousand babies are born in Milwaukee hospitals. COLE leaders met several times with Milwaukee health commissioner Jeanette Kowalik, who enthusiastically supported this proposal. We also met with key alderpersons. It became clear that we needed to start with a pilot project to test out the effectiveness and value of our proposal before it could go citywide. We decided to focus initially on the four zip codes with the highest density of lead poisoning in Milwaukee: 53204, 53206, 53208, and 53210. About twenty-four hundred babies are born each year from mothers who reside in these zip codes.

COLE convened a Lead-Free Summit at Hephatha in September 2019. The church was packed. Deanna Branch, a member of Hephatha, offered testimony about her experience as a mother whose five-year-old son, Aidan, is severely lead poisoned. COLE leaders presented the Birthing Moms Pilot Project and asked public officials to put $240,000 in Milwaukee's 2020 budget to provide free lead-education kits for twenty-four hundred birthing moms in the four targeted zip codes. Commissioner Kowalik and the five alderpersons present stood and publicly stated their commitment to do so. In the following month, several COLE leaders, including Deanna Branch, met with Mayor Barrett to elicit his support. COLE leaders attended the joint budget hearing of the common council and gave testimony. The Birthing Moms Pilot Project was fully funded in the 2020 budget.

Our success was significant, but it is just a start. Thirty-eight census tracts in Milwaukee show that at least 20 percent of children are lead poisoned. The effects of lead in paint, lead in water, and lead in soil continue to take a terrible toll. The costs of full lead abatement are daunting. State legislation places severe limitations on the legal ability of Milwaukee and other cities to adopt ordinances that could force landlords to remove sources of lead poisoning from rental properties. We will see what the future holds.

I keep in mind the questions posed by little Aidan to Commissioner Kowalik as people were gathering for the Lead-Free Summit. Aidan asked the commissioner, "Are you my friend?"

"Yes," she replied.

Then Aidan asked his second question: "Will you be my friend tomorrow?" That's a question awaiting a response from all of us in Milwaukee.

My pastor, the Rev. Mary Martha Kannass, has given the struggle for lead-free water a sacramental touch. The water in the aged building of Hephatha Lutheran Church is delivered through lead service lines. A few months into the organizing efforts of COLE, several children were baptized at Hephatha. Pastor Mary Martha poured water into the baptismal font from a certified lead filter water pitcher and announced: "For the first time in over one hundred years, children are being baptized with lead-free water from this font." Lead-free water has been poured into the font from a certified lead filter water pitcher for every baptism since that Sunday morning.

Pastor Mary Martha has also raised funds to distribute hundreds of certified lead filter water pitchers to mothers of infants and toddlers through the church's Strong Baby Sanctuary and at the neighboring public school. She connects the life-giving waters of baptism to her sacred care for the lives of children, both in the congregation and in the city.

Then the angel showed me the river of the water of life, bright as crystal, flowing from the throne of God and of the Lamb through the middle of the street of the city. (Rev 22:1–2)

Hagia Sophia (Gallery D)
11"x14" wood panel.
Egg tempera and gold leaf.

CHAPTER 6
Divine Feminine: *Sophia*

In this icon, Hagia Sophia (Holy Wisdom) reigns with the cosmos as her footstool. Her skin color is reddish due to the association of the Holy Spirit with fire. Encircling her head is an eight-pointed star (seven are visible) as reference to the future eon. The Trinity is numerically hinted: the throne rests on three visible legs, and three mandorlas of divine colors encompass her. Sophia speaks through the prophets and thus holds in her hand the prophetic scroll.

✧ ✧ ✧

I struggle with the patriarchal roots of congregation-based organizing of Saul Alinsky. I heard Alinsky speak on a couple of occasions, once while in college and once while in seminary. Alinsky was brilliant but also brash, rough, and in your face in a macho kind of way. I heard an Alinsky biographer say that if Alinsky were alive today, he wouldn't recognize what his organizing has become as it morphed into congregation-based organizing. That is mercifully true. And yet, despite the influence of the best faith-based values and of terrific female organizers and leaders,[1] congregation-based organizing still retains remnants of Alinsky's macho style.

For decades I have been uncomfortable and struggled with the patriarchal language used of God in Christianity. There is imbalance, limitation, domination, and gender exclusivity in imaging God as essentially Father, Son, and Holy Spirit (with the pronoun *he* being regularly applied in each instance). An exclusively male imaging of God has resulted in notions of God as king, warrior, and harsh judge; in the grim historical record of Christendom engaged in crusades, inquisitions, and witch burnings; and in male domination of church structures, ecclesial power, and the pulpit. When congregations frozen in exclusively male imaging of God, in male domination, and in a fundamentalist interpretation of Scripture engage in congregation-based organizing, the potential for the local organization to be a fully liberating force is severely limited. Pastors of these congregations may be heroically committed to racial and economic justice but often act in a way that diminishes women, disregards female leadership, and damns the LGBTQ community.

In contrast, social movements such as Black Lives Matter and the Women's March are breathtaking in their inclusivity, boldness, and liberative style. Might imaging God as Sophia—feminine, mysterious, and beyond gender—help us out here? I have to say that the more I read and reflect about Sophia, the more I am convinced of the power of Sophia to liberate and to enliven my thinking, praying, and acting as a Christian engaged in social justice.

---

1. See Susan Engh, *Women's Work: The Transformational Power of Faith-Based Community Organizing* (Lexington Books/Fortress Academic, 2019), for a remarkable tapestry of thoughtful reflections and stories of transformation from twenty-one women, including some of the finest congregation-based organizers in the country, who have exercised what Engh calls "lion-like courage" in the public arena.

I am deeply drawn to Sophia and have worked fairly hard at researching canonical Sophia iconography and drawing an icon pattern of her. For six months, the pattern sat on top of a mostly prepared gesso board, awaiting some movement on my part. I felt stuck. Who is Sophia in this icon? I could not proceed without some relatively satisfactory answer to this question. Of course, I knew that the process of painting Sophia was likely to deepen my understanding of her. But I didn't feel ready to start until I knew in what direction I was heading. Finally, I realized that the direction is toward an honoring of the Holy Spirit, who was named Sophia by some theologians in the early church. My reasons for equating Sophia with the Holy Spirit will be set forth below. While admitting that I am on shaky ground here in terms of canonical iconography, I decided to proceed and to paint the Sophia icon as a highly symbolic, nonrepresentational attempt to glorify the Holy Spirit—an attempt that is severely limited by my frailty and errors.

Sophia has entered my prayer life. Every morning I sing in the shower (to protect Lynn from my off-key voice) this adaptation of the ancient hymn "Creator Spirit, by Whose Aid":[2]

1. Sophia Spirit, by whose aid [original text: Creator Spirit, by whose aid]
The world's foundations first were laid,
Come, visit ev'ry humble mind;
Come, pour thy joys on humankind;
From sin and sorrow set us free,
And make thy temples fit for thee.

---

2. *Lutheran Book of Worship* (Minneapolis: Augsburg Publishing House and Philadelphia: Board of Publication, Lutheran Church in America, 1978), #164.

2. O Source of uncreated light,
The Father's promised Paraclete,
Thrice holy fount, thrice holy fire,
Our hearts with heav'nly love inspire;
Come and thy sacred unction bring
To sanctify us while we sing.

3. Plenteous of grace, descend from high
Rich in thy sev'n-fold energy;
Make us eternal truths receive
And practice all that we believe;
Give us thyself, that we may see
And love the Holy Trinity [original text: the Father and the Son by Thee].

I recall the evaluation session directly following a dynamic public meeting of one thousand MICAH leaders in Milwaukee when Mike Kruglik, a seasoned Gamaliel organizer, asked, "Did anyone not feel the presence of the Holy Spirit tonight?" I agree with Mike. Sophia was definitely present and inspiring us that evening.

My awareness of the divine and my prayer life have been broadened and deepened by extensive time in retirement enjoying nature. For much of my life, I have associated Christ with human struggle, human suffering, and human liberation. From the perspective of sitting in my kayak on a lake gazing at pine forest and soaring birds, the liberating Christ of Dietrich Bonhoeffer, Martin Luther King Jr., and others summons forth the best of me but also feels limited to the human dimension. The cosmic, fiery, life-generating primal energy of the Holy Spirit or Sophia feels equally vital. In an age of catastrophic climate change, I am especially mindful of "God's Grandeur" by Gerard Manley Hopkins (1844–1889):

> And for all this, nature is never spent;
> There lives the dearest freshness deep down things;
> And though the last lights off the black West went
>   Oh, morning, at the brown brink eastward, springs—
> Because the Holy Ghost over the bent
>   World broods with warm breast and with ah! bright wings.[3]

The human journey, as important as it is, is of little consequence to the cosmos, somewhat like a speck of sand on a vast ocean beach. Sophia, existing outside of time and also within time, generates energy, matter, and life throughout the cosmos; constructs the mathematical formulas foundational to all things; guides evolutionary activity in geological time and in human history; breathes physical and eternal life into the human soul; and creates friends of God and prophets. I have only a cloudy, miniscule glimpse of all this, and yet I am awestruck.

Sophia is a Greek word that translates as "wisdom" in English. Sophia is personified in several passages of the Septuagint, the earliest extant Greek translation of the Hebrew Bible, and of several apocryphal writings such as the Wisdom of Solomon (canonical for Roman Catholics). Here are several of my favorite Sophia passages:

---

3. Gerard Manley Hopkins, *Poems of Gerard Manley Hopkins*, ed. Robert Bridges (London: Humphrey Milford, 1918). Originally written in 1877.

Does not wisdom [Sophia] call, and does not understanding raise her voice? . . . The Lord created me at the beginning of his work, the first of his acts of long ago. Ages ago I was set up, at the first, before the beginning of the earth. When there were no depths I was brought forth, when there were no springs abounding with water. . . . then I was beside him, like a master worker; and I was daily his delight, rejoicing before him always. (Prov 8:1, 22–24, 30)

For wisdom [Sophia] is more mobile than any motion; because of her pureness she pervades and penetrates all things. For she is a breath of the power of God, and a pure emanation of the glory of the Almighty; therefore nothing defiled gains entrance into her. For she is a reflection of eternal light, a spotless mirror of the working of God, and an image of his goodness. Although she is but one, she can do all things, and while remaining in herself, she renews all things; in every generation she passes into holy souls and makes them friends of God and prophets. (Wis 7:24–27)

A holy people and blameless race wisdom [Sophia] delivered from a nation of oppressors . . . she guided them along a marvelous way, and became a shelter to them by day, and a starry flame through the night. She brought them over the Red Sea, and led them through deep waters. (Wis 10:15, 17–18)

Scholarly study of Sophia by the theologian Elizabeth Johnson results in this conclusion:

> Given the immediate religious context of the wisdom texts, namely, Jewish monotheism not amenable to the idea of

more than one God, the idea that Sophia is Israel's God in female imagery is most reasonable. Rabbinic specialists themselves argue that neither wisdom nor word, neither God's name nor Spirit nor the *shekinah* were introduced into Judaism as secondary hypostases to offset the utter transcendence of the divine. Rather, these are ways of asserting the one, transcendent God's nearness to the world in such a way that divine transcendence is not compromised. Consequently, to say that Sophia is the fashioner of all things, that she delivered Israel from a nation of oppressors, or that her gifts are justice and life is to speak of the transcendent God's relation to the world, of *God's* nearness, activity, and summons. Accordingly, the Wisdom of God in Jewish thought is simply God, revealing and known.[4]

The early church knew Sophia, and several theologians began to see her as an extension of the Godhead. Theophilus of Antioch (second century CE), the first theologian known to use the word *Trinity*, spoke of the Logos and Sophia as the two hands of God in the creation of human beings: "When God said, 'Let us make [man] after our image and likeness'. . . he regarded the making of [man] as the only work worthy of his own hands . . . [and] he said, 'Let us make' to none other than his own Logos and his own Sophia."[5]

Irenaeus of Lyons (second century CE) also included Sophia in the metaphor of the two hands of God:

---

4. Elizabeth A. Johnson, *She Who Is* (New York: Crossroad, 1994), 91–92.
5. Theophilus of Antioch, to Autolycus, 2.18, as cited by Madonna S. Compton, *The Divine Sophia* (Berkeley and Kansas City: The Raphael Group, 2013), Kindle version, Loc 487.

> For God did not stand in need of these [beings], in order to the accomplishing of what He had Himself determined with Himself beforehand should be done, as if He did not possess His own hands. For with Him were always present the Word and Wisdom, the Son and the Spirit, by whom and in whom, freely and spontaneously, He made all things.[6]

Irenaeus clearly identified Sophia with the Holy Spirit:

> as the prophet also says: by the word of the Lord the heavens were established, and all the power of them by His Spirit [Psalm 33:6]. Hence, since the Word 'establishes' that is, works bodily and consolidates being, while the Spirit disposes and shapes the various 'powers,' so the Word is fitly and properly called the Son, but the Spirit the Wisdom of God.[7]

Why did Sophia fade as a name for the Holy Spirit? Perhaps to protect the church from confusion with Egyptian and Greek goddess cults. Perhaps as defense against gnostic devotion to Sophia. Perhaps because the attributes of Sophia were transferred to Christ, "the wisdom of God" (1 Cor 1:24). Perhaps, and perhaps most likely, because men in power preferred a masculine conception of God.

✧ ✧ ✧

---

6. St. Irenaeus of Lyons, *Against Heresies*, ed. Paul A. Böer (Veritas Splendor Publications, Kindle Edition, 2012), Book IV, Chapter 20, paragraph 1.

7. St. Irenaeus of Lyons, *Proof of the Apostolic Preaching*, trans. Joseph P. Smith, S.J. (Westminster, MD: The Newman Press, 1952), section A, paragraph 5.

O power of Wisdom
You encompassed the cosmos
encircling and embracing all
in one living orbit

with your three wings:
one soars on high
one distills the earth essence
and the third hovers everywhere.[8]

Thomas Merton was devoted to Sophia and spoke of her poetically:

Perhaps in a certain very primitive aspect Sophia is
the unknown, the dark, the nameless Ousia. Perhaps
she is even the Divine Nature, One in Father, Son, and
Holy Ghost. And perhaps she is in infinite light unmanifest,
not even waiting to be known as Light. This I do not know.
Out of the silence Light is spoken. We do not hear it or see
it until it is spoken.[9]

I am awestruck before you, Sophia.

I grow silent and simply sit in my prayer hut while you envelop me with the warmth of your love, and your uncreated light glows in my inner darkness.

---

8. Hildegard of Bingen, quoted in Barbara Newman, *Sister of Wisdom: St. Hildegard's Theology of the Feminine* (Berkeley: University of California Press, 1989), 64.

9. Thomas Merton, *Hagia Sophia*, "III. High Morning. The Hour of Tierce," https://www.poeticous.com/thomas-merton/hagia-sophia.

My kayak glides slowly through shimmering river water, and I see the hint of you in a treetop eagle, in the flight of a great blue heron, in the bordering birch and pine forest, in a cloud flowing sky. Hiking, I enter the geological time of a Utah canyon, and I see that I am as nothing, and you are all and beyond all.

In worship, I watch in wonder as a mother gently comforts her teenaged daughter who is using a wheelchair, damaged in brain and body since birth, crying out now and then in pain, methodically twirling a cloth—her praise dance. And I think: this is your mothering, your comforting, and your pain. *Finitum capax infiniti.*

In naming the Holy Spirit as Sophia, I need to be clear that I do so both mindful of and deeply affirming of the caveat of St. Augustine:

> All speaking of God, he [Augustine] insists, must be born out of silence and ignorance and return there, for God is ineffable. We give God many names but ultimately God is nameless, no name being able to express the divine nature. . . . In the end, it is easier to say what God is not than what God is: If you have understood, then this is not God. If you were able to understand, then you understand something else instead of God. If you were able to understand even partially, then you have deceived yourself with your own thoughts.[10]

---

10. Elizabeth A. Johnson, *She Who Is* (New York: Crossroad, 1992), 108. (Referencing Augustine, *Sermon* 52, c.1, n.16.)

Acheiropoietos ("made without hands") (Gallery E) 11"x14" wood panel. Egg tempera and gold leaf.

CHAPTER 7
Holy Faces: *Acheiropoietos*

Whose face do I see? When I am engaged in organizing for justice, do I simply see the issues and the actions, or do I see the faces of the immigrants, the children, the prisoners, and the unemployed directly affected by these issues and actions? Am I blinded by my own need to be seen and to be recognized? Does my ego block out the faces of others? Why does it matter at all to me whether my face appears on television or in a newspaper because of a public action?

How many faces can I see? I see the faces of those whom I love and who love me, concentric circles of beloved faces: family, friends, mentors, companions in the struggle and in the journey. I cannot imagine losing those faces. I dread the power of death to take those faces away from me. I have no interest in some disembodied heaven where faces no longer matter. But how many faces can I really see? I'm an introvert. There are limits to my capacity for relationships. My compassion has its limits as well. I can see the face of someone with whom I am engaged one-on-one. I can walk a bit with one formerly incarcerated person or with one person seeking a job. I can see them. But when there are thousands of formerly incarcerated or unemployed persons in Milwaukee, I end up seeing masses and not individual faces. I cannot see the trees for the forest. And yet, who am I if I don't?

As to seeing the face of God, this is a dicey business: "My heart says, 'seek his face!' Your face, Lord, do I seek" (Ps 27:8). "But," he said, "you cannot see my face; for no one shall see me and live" (Exod 33:20). We seek that which we cannot see. God's face, symbolic of God's essence, is hidden from us in this life. As to the next life, I am not sure.

Perhaps seeing the face of God is a matter of friendship and purity: "Thus the Lord used to speak to Moses face to face, as one speaks to a friend" (Exod 33:11). "Blessed are the pure in heart, for they will see God" (Matt 5:8). I lack purity of heart. I am not God's friend. I will never see the face of God in this life. As to the next life, perhaps I will catch a glimpse. Perhaps. It is, after all, a matter of pure grace and promise: "They will see his face, and his name will be on their foreheads" (Rev 22:4). We'll see.

Where do we see the face of Christ in this life? Can I see Christ without seeing the face of Christ in my neighbor who is in need? "Then the righteous will answer him, 'Lord, when was it that we saw you hungry and gave you food, or thirsty and gave you something to drink? And when was it that we saw you a stranger and welcomed you, or naked and gave you clothing? And when was it that we saw you sick or in prison and visited you?' And the king will answer them, 'Truly I tell you, just as you did it to one of the least of these who are members of my family, you did it to me'" (Matt 25:37–40).

It is instructive that in the parable of the last judgment, neither the righteous nor the unrighteous recognize the Son of Man in the faces of those in need. Both reply, "When did we see you?" To the unrighteous this would be a matter of indifference, except that their eternal destiny is now on the line. To the righteous, what mattered most was not their salvation or correct religious living. They were not trying to prove their worth or rack up points. They simply saw the face of a human being in need and responded compassionately. The faithful response is not motivated by religious impulse or by a desire to please God. Compassion is the motivation. Perhaps later we will realize that when we saw a brother or sister in the face of the one we helped, we were also seeing the face of Christ.

The icon *Acheiropoietos* ("made without hands") depicts the face of Christ Jesus on a cloth. In the Orthodox tradition, this icon has its mysterious origins in the legend of King Abgar of Edessa, who lived during the time of Jesus. In one version, King Abgar suffered from leprosy. Hearing that Jesus had great power to heal, King Abgar sent two of his officials to Jesus with a letter humbly seeking healing. Moved by the letter, Jesus pressed his face to a cloth and gave it to the officials to take back to Abgar. When Abgar unwrapped the cloth, he saw a miraculous image of the face of Jesus and was instantly healed of his leprosy.

Leprosy, medically known as Hansen's disease, is a chronic bacterial infection that attacks nerve endings, particularly those in the hands, feet, and face. The result is a loss of sensation in those areas, putting a person at much greater risk of injury as they cannot feel pain. Without the ability to feel pain, people injure themselves, and the injuries can become infected, resulting in tissue loss.

I think that there is a form of leprosy that is rampant in our country. This leprosy is a kind of spiritual mirror image of Hansen's disease in which one still feels one's own pain but has become incapable of feeling the pain of others. The body politic is afflicted. A psychic numbing becomes rampant. The nation has become indifferent to the pain of millions of refugees, to the daily suffering of those trapped in concentrated poverty, to children whose lives are cut short by our drones and air strikes, and to species made extinct by environmental ruin of our making.

I struggle for healing from this leprosy. Over the course of decades of urban ministry, I became numb to the horror stories that surrounded me. All too often, I felt nothing or very little when learning of yet another killing in the neighborhood of the church. Sometimes, my humanity surfaced through the leprosy. A young woman in my congregation somehow concealed her out-of-wedlock pregnancy from her mother and then suffocated the baby when it was born in her bed. The mother was jailed and later sentenced to prison. The baby was contained in a tiny open coffin in a funeral home. After the brief memorial service, I went to my car, sat down, and screamed.

But usually the leprosy prevailed. A week before my retirement, I got a phone call at dawn from a member of the congregation letting me know that there had been a homicide on the street outside of the church office. A drug deal had gone bad. The sellers and buyers drew weapons on each other. One of the out-of-town buyers was chased down the street and shot repeatedly. He ran a little farther and then collapsed on the street in front of my office. When I arrived, the police were gone, and so was the body. A chalk silhouette of the body marked the spot of his death a few yards from my office. I felt nothing. My leprosy numbed the pain.

The image of Christ's face healed King Abgar of his leprosy. I gaze at the *Acheiropoietos* icon and pray for the healing of mine.

✧ ✧ ✧

Spiritual leprosy also distorts the human face, so honest and genuine in babies and small children, and twists it into a deceptive mask. In ancient Greek theater, the persona was a theatrical mask worn by an actor to portray a character being dramatized. We all learn to wear our own persona (perhaps we have many such masks) in order to survive and advance in society. We wear these masks before others in order to conceal our true selves. Over time, our true selves are concealed even from us. We no longer know who we truly are.

One Latin word for mask is *larva*, which carried the meaning in ancient times of "ghost." A mask is a face without life in it: a ghost rather than a true spirit. The one in whom the image of God has become concealed by a mask becomes ghostly, without authentic substance. A mask bears shadow, emptiness, and darkness. A mask hides the truth and conveys false reality. Politicians are particularly adept at wearing masks, but this spiritual leprosy afflicts us all. We see the mask all around us. We see the mask in ourselves. How different is our inner pain and insecurity from what we project to the world? How different is the private unfaithfulness within us from the pietistic mask we present in public?

I recall visiting a fifteen-year-old in the Milwaukee Children's Detention Center who had worshipped on several occasions at the church I served. He was awaiting trial for murdering a woman in a shopping mall parking lot as her five-year-old daughter watched in horror. His intent was to rob the woman. When the police asked him why he fired his shotgun, he simply said, "Because she smiled at me." This boy's classmates described him as friendly and kind—a good student. To all appearances, that is who he was. He seemed gentle, quiet, and respectful to me. He also showed no remorse. I left the detention center thinking that he had no clue as to what he had done or who he was. The mask was firmly in place. Surely prison would add mask upon mask.

In ancient Greek, one word for slave was *aprosopos*, "the one without a face." In the brutality of our society, which so devalues the human spirit and so glorifies what produces wealth, the poor and the expendable are made to feel as if they have no face, no identity, no point of recognition. Aprosopos continues to be the experience of most African Americans when entering white society, mostly unchanged since Ralph Ellison's powerful indictment in his book, *The Invisible Man*. "I am an invisible man," Ellison says in his prologue. "When they approach me they see only my surroundings, themselves, or figments of their imagination—indeed, everything and anything except me."[1]

What is the point of gazing at an icon of the face of Christ if the faces of others remain invisible to me?

How might I remove my mask and rediscover my true face? The story is told that St. Seraphim of Sarov, a beloved Russian mystic of the early nineteenth century, once had a conversation with his disciple Motovilov in the clearing of a forest on a winter morning. When Motovilov asked St. Seraphim about the purpose of the Christian life, "the monk Seraphim answered that 'it is the

---

1. Ralph Ellison, *Invisible Man* (New York: Vintage International, 1995), 3.

acquisition of the Holy Spirit.' 'But what does this mean?' Motovilov persisted. 'Look at me,' Seraphim said to him simply. Then Motovilov saw his friend standing in the snow with his face shining like the sun."[2]

In the Western tradition of the *Acheiropoietos* icon, Veronica (*vera ikon*, "true icon") is moved by compassion to leave the safety of the crowd of spectators in order to offer some comfort to Jesus as he stumbles while carrying the cross on the way to Golgotha. She presses a cloth to his face to wipe his blood and sweat. The cloth miraculously changes to contain an image of the face of Jesus. Those who risk their safety and their lives in acts of mercy and justice for those who are afflicted are blessed with the presence of Christ.

But what about the spectator, the bystander, the one who looks on but stays put? In one of my devotional books, I keep a letter that Phil Berrigan sent me during one of his prison stays for resisting nuclear weapons. In typically strong, prophetic language, Phil warns against becoming a bystander in a world of "spiritual dislocation, moral paralysis, epidemic war and ethnic bloodshed, global pollution, corporate supremacy, usury and profit grubbing, urbanization, drug consumption, vapidity of religion, foolhardy biological research."[3]

In contradistinction to the courageous compassion of Veronica, consider the bystander in Phil's description:

> In so much of human experience we are forced to distinguish among the victims, the victimizers, and the

---

2. *The Living God: A Catechism for the Christian Faith, Volume 1*, trans. Olga Dunlop (Crestwood, NY: St. Vladimir's Seminary Press, 1989), 90.
3. Philip Berrigan, personal letter to the author, March 1, 1998.

bystanders. The bystanders are the most curious; they are the ordinary human article who stay home—safe enough if compliant enough. They can't be charged with taking part in any evil act; they watch as evil proceeds. They create the norm, define what is common. When a whole population takes on the status of bystander, the victims are without allies. How is it that indifference, which on its own does no apparent harm, ends up by washing itself in the very horrors it means to have nothing to do with? The act of turning toward—while carrying a club or gun or bomb—is an act of brutality; but the act of turning away, however empty-handed and harmlessly, remains an act. Indifference grows lethal.[4]

On this icon, you may see a thin gash extending horizontally from the chin of Jesus. I first noticed this damage following a break-in that occurred in the parsonage when I served as pastor of Trinity Lutheran Church in a tough neighborhood of Jersey City. I guess that whoever broke in didn't like the icon and decided to leave his mark. At first I was upset. But gradually I came to realize that in some ways, the gash makes the icon more real and down to earth. After all, Jesus didn't live in a parsonage and didn't have the privileged status of clergy. His friends included tax collectors and sinners. Judas stole from the money bag that Jesus entrusted to him. Jesus was crucified between two bandits. One mocked him. To the other, Jesus promised eternal life. I pray eternal life for the thief who gashed this icon. Perhaps if I lost my privilege and was in desperation, I too might break in and steal.

---

4. Philip Berrigan, personal letter to the author, March 1, 1998.

CHAPTER 8
Angelic Power: *Archangel Michael*

Archangel Michael (Gallery F)
11"x14" wood panel.
Egg tempera and gold leaf.

The Archangel Michael, protector of the Israelites (Dan 12:1) and victorious in heavenly battle against the dragon Satan (Rev 12:7–9), is depicted holding a lance in his right hand and a transparent blue sphere in his left; Michael belongs to the sphere of the divine life centered in Christ (ICXC). "Over all the Nine Ranks of Angels, the Lord appointed the Holy Archangel Michael (his name in Hebrew means 'who is like unto God'), the faithful servitor of God, as Chief Commander. He cast down from Heaven the arrogantly proud Lucifer and the other fallen spirits when they rebelled against God. Michael summoned the ranks of angels and cried out, 'Let us attend! Let us stand aright before our Creator and do not consider doing what is displeasing unto God!'"[1]

❖ ❖ ❖

Does the Archangel Michael exist? In an age dominated by a purely materialist view of reality, belief in angels seems anachronistic and

---

1. Orthodox Church in America, "Synaxis of the Archangel Michael and the Other Bodiless Powers," https://www.oca.org/saints/lives/2020/11/08/103244-synaxis-of-the-archangel-michael-and-the-other-bodiless-powers.

naive. Nevertheless, Michael figures strongly in the sacred writings of Judaism, Christianity, and Islam:

> At that time Michael, the great prince, the protector of your people, shall arise. There shall be a time of anguish, such as has never occurred since nations first came into existence. (Dan 12:1)

> And war broke out in heaven; Michael and his angels fought against the dragon. The dragon and his angels fought back, but they were defeated, and there was no longer any place for them in heaven. (Rev 12:7–8)

> Whoever is an enemy of God and His angels and His message-bearers, including Gabriel and Michael, [should know that,] verily, God is the enemy of all who deny the truth. (Surah 2:98, *The Message of the Qur'an*, translated by Muhammad Asad)

The *Archangel Michael* icon reminds us that heavenly forces lead and uphold the people of God in the ongoing struggle against oppression and evil. When our efforts at organizing and struggling for justice seem hopeless, dismal, and quixotic, we especially need to remember that we are not on our own.

Consider the story of Elisha being hunted down by the army of the king of Aram. The army locates the prophet in the town of Dothan and encircles it. To the eye that sees only the material realm, Elisha is doomed:

> When an attendant of the man of God rose early in the morning and went out, an army with horses and chariots was all around the city. His servant said, "Alas, master! What shall we do?" He replied, "Do not be afraid, for

there are more with us than there are with them." Then Elisha prayed: "O Lord, please open his eyes that he may see." So the Lord opened the eyes of the servant, and he saw; the mountain was full of horses and chariots of fire all around Elisha. (2 Kgs 6:15–17)

Similarly, Jesus sees more than the large crowd armed with swords and clubs that has come to arrest him in the garden of Gethsemane:

> Then they came and laid hands on Jesus and arrested him. Suddenly, one of those with Jesus put his hand on his sword, drew it, and struck the slave of the high priest, cutting off his ear. Then Jesus said to him, "Put your sword back into its place; for all who take the sword will perish by the sword. Do you think that I cannot appeal to my Father, and he will at once send me more than twelve legions of angels?" (Matt 26:50–53)

Then there is the kitchen table experience of Rev. Martin Luther King Jr. In January 1956, one month into the Montgomery bus boycott, King was arrested and jailed for the first time under the pretext that he was speeding—driving thirty miles an hour in a twenty-five-mile-an-hour speed zone. On the way to jail, King was convinced that he was being set up to be lynched. The pressure continued upon his release. Martin and Coretta received an onslaught of phone calls in their home, spewing racist abuse and death threats. On some days, they contended with as many as forty such calls.

On January 27, 1956, King came home from a strategy meeting, exhausted and emotionally worn from another long day. The phone rang. King picked up the receiver only to hear an ugly voice threatening death if King did not leave Montgomery. In his book *Stride toward Freedom*, King recalls what happened next:

> I got out of bed and began to walk the floor. Finally I went to the kitchen and heated a pot of coffee. I was ready to give up. With my cup of coffee sitting untouched before me I tried to think of a way to move out of the picture without appearing a coward. In this state of exhaustion, when my courage had all but gone, I decided to take my problem to God. With my head in my hands, I bowed over the kitchen table and prayed aloud. The words I spoke to God that midnight are still vivid in my memory. "I am here taking a stand for what I believe is right. But now I am afraid. The people are looking to me for leadership, and if I stand before them without strength and courage, they too will falter. I am at the end of my powers. I have nothing left. I've come to the point where I can't face it alone."
>
> At that moment I experienced the presence of the Divine as I had never experienced Him before. It seemed as though I could hear the quiet assurance of an inner voice saying: "Stand up for righteousness, stand up for truth; and God will be at your side forever." Almost at once my fears began to go. My uncertainty disappeared. I was ready to face anything.[2]

Three days later, King's wife, Coretta, and their baby narrowly escaped death when a bomb blast rocked their house. King recalled, "Strangely enough, I accepted the word of the bombing

---

2. Martin Luther King Jr., *Stride toward Freedom* (Boston: Beacon, 1958, 1986), 124–25.

calmly. My religious experience a few nights before had given me the strength to face it."³

✧ ✧ ✧

On September 9, 1980, Daniel Berrigan and seven other Christian peace activists entered the General Electric nuclear weapons facility in King of Prussia, Pennsylvania, and enacted the "swords into plowshares" prophecy of Isaiah 2:4 by taking hammers to Mark-12A nuclear warhead nose cones and pouring blood on documents and files. I headed the defense committee for the Plowshares Eight. Following their conviction and sentencing, Dan sent me this poem in which I think he poetically touches on the intersection of the spiritual and material realms in prophetic action:

> "for the first anniversary of plowshares eight"
> Everything enhances, everything
> gives glory, everything.
> Between bark and bite
> Judge Salus's undermined soul
> betrays him, mutters
> very alleluias. The iron cells—
> row on row of rose trellised
> mansions, bridal chambers!
> Curses, vans, keys, guards—behold
> the imperial lions of our vast acres!
> And when hammers come down
> and our years are tossed to four winds—
> why, confetti blinds the eye, the saints
> pelt us with flowers! For every hour

---

3. King, *Stride toward Freedom*, 126.

scant with discomfort
(the mastiff's baleful eye, the bailiff's mastery)
see, the Lord's hands heap
eon upon eon
like fruit bowls at a feast.[4]

One evening my wife, Lynn, and I visited with Daniel Berrigan in his apartment on the upper west side of Manhattan. (It was my great honor and delight to visit with Dan almost weekly in those days.) I gave Dan an icon of the *Archangel Michael* that I had painted in a class taught by the master iconographer Vladislav Andrejev. Here's an excerpt from a letter that followed:

> Dear Lynn and Jake,
>
> I'm still in the glow of your presence, and the presence of your extraordinary gift, which seem to come to the same light, shed by both you and the ikon. Surely St. Michael is the most powerful person to enter here since you left; I can only stammer my thank you, with all my heart. Given this Advent and its mysterious goings on, an angel is much to be invoked and welcomed. Michael is still looking over the walls for an appropriate place from which to view everything, including illegal propensities and likelihoods . . .
>
> Love,
> Daniel[5]

---

4. Daniel Berrigan, "Swords into Plowshares," in *The Sign of Peace: Journal of the Catholic Peace Fellowship* 7.1 (2008): 31. Used with the author's permission.
5. Daniel Berrigan, personal letter to the author.

In the book of Daniel, the Archangel Michael is seen as protecting the exiled Jews and contending against the princely angel of the Persians. Spiritual forces of justice and goodness are in constant resistance against spiritual forces of empire and domination. The apostle Paul reminds us that "our struggle is not against enemies of blood and flesh, but against the rulers, against the authorities, against the cosmic powers of this present darkness, against the spiritual forces of evil in the heavenly places" (Eph 6:12).

In a modern age, we are a bit embarrassed by this kind of imagery. But anyone who has really struggled against evil and oppression knows that there is more here than meets the eye. There are dimensions to racism and violence and materialism that cannot be fully explained by sociology or psychology. Evil exists and is more than the sum of its parts. In organizing, we quickly learn that victories in the public arena are always relative and tentative due to the unyielding nature of principalities and powers, and that the forces of domination against which we struggle all too often show up in ourselves. Within each of us is a spiritual battleground, and this battleground is projected into the public arena in profound and disheartening ways. That is one reason prayer, liturgy, and confession need to be essential practices for those engaged in congregation-based organizing.

Bill Wylie-Kellermann is the foremost living theologian of the principalities and powers. For decades, Bill has struggled and organized valiantly in Detroit against the greed of multinational auto companies and banking systems, racist gentrification, ruinous government, and water shutoffs in poor neighborhoods. While engaging in savvy organizing, Bill understands these forces theologically as principalities and powers, and he consequently weaves liturgical, symbolic action into nonviolent resistance against them. Bill seeks a deep understanding of the spiritual forces at work in the city that he loves and over which he agonizes: "After the biblical manner of the angels of the nations (portrayed most dramatically in Daniel 10) or the angels of the churches (addressed in the opening chapters of Revelation), I have begun to speak of the 'angel of Detroit.' The term piques and intrigues. By it I mean what has been called the 'actual inner spirituality' of the city. I mean to get at its identity and vocation, its character and personality, its potentiality as well as its fallenness before God."[6]

One of the items on my fireplace mantle is an art piece created by Dan Berrigan. A cutout of the prophet Daniel sits glumly inside a barred, black jail cell constructed of wood. Also in the cell is a tiny, beaded angel who sits on the back of a wooden lion. The years have taken their toll. Some of the beads of which the angel is made have fallen off, so the angel is slumped over and looks a little worn. A fall from the fireplace mantle broke a couple of the cell bars. I started to replace them but then thought better. Why not allow Daniel and his angel an escape route? Perhaps the angels will do the same for me and my loved ones someday.

---

6. Bill Wylie-Kellermann, *Principalities in Particular* (Minneapolis: Fortress, 2017), 87.

St. Francis and the Sultan (Gallery G)
11"x14" wood panel.
Egg tempera and gold leaf.

CHAPTER 9

God Is Greater: St. Francis and the Sultan

In 1219, amid the horrors of the Fifth Crusade, St. Francis crossed enemy lines to gain an audience with al-Malik al-Kamil, the sultan of Egypt, in his camp on the banks of the Nile.[1] Francis probably hoped to end the warfare by converting the sultan from Islam to Christianity. The sultan extended remarkable hospitality to the monk and offered him many gifts. Francis accepted one: the gift of an ivory horn.

One of the more profound spiritual journeys of my life was a visit to Assisi, where I was confronted by the radical simplicity of Francis and Clare and by their total devotion to Christ. (St. Clare of Assisi and Francis were friends who deeply influenced each other. Clare founded the Poor Clares as the Second Order of St. Francis.) In the room of relics accessed through the lower church of the Basilica of St. Francis, I saw the ivory horn, which al-Malik al-Kamil gave to Francis. Legend has it that Francis used the ivory horn as a call to prayer.

I decided to paint an icon titled *St. Francis and the Sultan* as a means of drawing closer to the remarkable peacemaking of Francis

---

1. See Paul Moses, *The Saint and the Sultan* (New York: Random House, 2009).

and to the openheartedness of al-Malik al-Kamil. Amid the tragic, often horrific hostilities between Christians and Muslims, the icon seeks to portray a hopeful encounter and a path to peace.

I placed a small olive tree between and behind al-Malik-al-Kamil and Francis. An olive branch is a symbol of peace. But the tree is small, and the setting is barren. Will the tree grow? Is peace a possibility? The encounter between Francis and al-Malik-al-Kamil did not stop the Crusades. And yet their openness to each other surely suggests a different path than the road to perdition currently being taken in our day.

I decided not to put a halo on al-Malik-al-Kamil. I thought it insulting to Christianize him. I also chose to emphasize the gift of the ivory horn from the sultan rather than the proclamation of the gospel by the saint. I suppose that this icon may violate canonical iconography, but I don't think we can get anywhere in Muslim-Christian relations unless we are willing to cross boundaries, take risks, and openly encounter each other in the spirit of al-Malik-al-Kamil and Francis.

One of the gifts of congregation-based organizing is that it is interfaith. Many of these organizations include in their membership Christians, Muslims, Jews, and Unitarians. Some include an even wider range of faith traditions. In a time of religious hostility, suspicion, ignorance, and sectarianism, a grassroots organization that is interfaith is a symbol of hope and an embodiment of a new way of living together.

I also think that Christians can often try the patience of their interfaith partners. I recall a meeting of MICAH's Religious Leaders Caucus when the chairperson, normally a considerate and sensitive pastor, was annoyed and shot a dirty look when an imam's cell phone sounded a ringtone in the middle of the meeting. The ringtone was simply reminding the imam that it was time for prayer.

It took years for MICAH to stop scheduling events on the Sabbath, and a number of preachers, including top leaders, simply could not stop praying in the name of Jesus at public meetings. At last we agreed that whoever led public prayers that were not inclusive would at least offer a brief introduction to the effect that they were praying from their tradition. I still think this is hard on Muslims, Jews, and Unitarians. All too often the claim to be interfaith is in reality a reference to an organization that is dominated by Christians and lacks authentic sensitivity or appreciation for other faith traditions. The message is a bit like saying, "You are welcome in my house. By the way, don't forget that it is my house."

And yet the gift of the ivory horn remains—a lovely gesture across boundaries made possible by mutual respect, perhaps even friendship. Congregation-based organizing, despite all its blemishes, remains a rare opportunity at the grassroots level for people of goodwill from a wide range of belief systems to struggle collectively for justice even as they struggle to appreciate and to value their differences. Throughout the United States, in all of the national faith-based organizing networks, congregation-based organizations like MICAH are forging, with trial and error, new models of the beloved community.

Here is a personal confession: I still struggle with my own tendency to think of Christianity as superior to other world religions. Perhaps this has much to do with my growing up as a Missouri Synod Lutheran with a fundamentalist myopia. How do I live out a clear commitment to Christ while at the same time honoring the deep value of other ancient belief systems? My daughter Nora is a scholar and professor in Islamic studies. Her husband, Wajdi, now a PhD candidate, grew up in a Muslim culture in Tunisia. Nora lovingly challenges me when I exhibit a Christian bias and patiently helps me to grow in my appreciation and understanding of Islam. Wajdi knows the harsh historical connection between missional Christendom and Western imperialism and yet is respectful and inquisitive of my faith. In my reading, I realize that I am learning more from some of the Sufi saints and mystics than I have learned from most of their Christian counterparts. I am also learning that Islam, like Christianity, is an incredibly rich and complicated tapestry. I am a novice. But I am trying to learn.

As I write these words, I am overjoyed that I will soon be a grandfather to Tameem. I pray for Tameem, and I hope that he will grow up in a context that honors and celebrates him for who he is and for who he will become, regardless of his ethnicity or skin color or language or religion or lack of religion. Tameem will surely help me to continue to grow. Love can do no other.

Religion without humanity is a poor human stuff. (Sojourner Truth)[2]

If I make my religion an obstacle between me and you, I also make it an obstacle between me and God. (Traditional saying)

---

2. Olive Gilbert, Frances W. Titus, and Susan B. Anthony Collection, *Narrative of Sojourner Truth: A Bondswoman of Olden Time* (Battle Creek, MI: Published for the author, 1884), 26.

✧ ✧ ✧

What is an idol? Any god *who is mine but not yours*, any god concerned with me but not with you, *is an idol*.[3] (Rabbi Abraham Joshua Heschel)

✧ ✧ ✧

We believe in that which has been bestowed from on high upon us, as well as that which has been bestowed upon you: for our God and your God is one and the same, and it is unto Him that we [all] surrender ourselves.[4] (Surah 29:46)

✧ ✧ ✧

We are here to awaken from our illusion of separateness.[5] (Thich Nhat Hanh)

✧ ✧ ✧

The primary confession of the Christian before the world is the deed, which interprets itself . . . the deed alone is our confession of faith before the world.[6] (Dietrich Bonhoeffer)

---

3. Rabbi Abraham Joshua Heschel, "Religion and Race" (1963), paragraph 11, https://voicesofdemocracy.umd.edu/heschel-religion-and-race-speech-text/. The entire text was originally printed in *The Insecurity of Freedom* (New York: Farrar, Straus and Giroux, 1966), 85–100.
4. *The Message of the Qur'an*, translated by Muhammad Asad (Bristol: Book Foundation, 2003), 684–85.
5. Thich Nhat Hanh Foundation, "What We Fund," https://thichnhathanhfoundation.org/what-we-fund.
6. Dietrich Bonhoeffer, *A Testament to Freedom*, eds. Geffrey B. Kelly and F. Burton Nelson (San Francisco: Harper, 1995), 86.

St. George and the Dragon (Gallery H)
11"x14" wood panel.
Egg tempera and gold leaf.

CHAPTER 10
Inner Harmony: *St. George and the Dragon*

Vladislav Andrejev, master iconographer and founder of the Prosopon School of Iconology, taught me that the legend of St. George and the Dragon can be understood as an allegory of the spiritual struggle for wholeness. The dragon represents those egoistic impulses of the flesh, which are boundless in their demanding appetite and ultimately will devour the soul (represented by the princess). St. George rides a white horse (symbolizing the spirit) to rescue the soul (princess). In this version of the icon *St. George and the Dragon*, the dragon is subdued, not slain, by the cross and is leashed in service of the soul (princess). The result is wholeness—an integrated harmony of spirit, soul, and flesh.

✧ ✧ ✧

Many people deny the existence of the soul and claim that we are simply fleshy machines. Most Christian believers, unless they are from an Orthodox tradition, are hard-pressed to articulate a difference between spirit and soul. As to the flesh, well, that is quite well known by everyone. Perhaps, especially in our materialistic, capitalist society, the dragon has already devoured us.

✧ ✧ ✧

The legend of St. George and the Dragon suggests a spiritual struggle that is simultaneously engaged both within and without. The question of self-interest is vital both to the inner struggle for wholeness and to the outer struggle for justice. Why am I involved in this or that cause or issue campaign? What motivates me? Is it guilt? Is it a need to prove myself? Is the public arena a way of avoiding my inner boredom or emotional pain? Am I trying to be some kind of savior? If I do not reflect honestly on these and other questions, I run the risk of enslaving myself even as I work for the liberation of others. Congregation-based organizing offers deep opportunities for harmonious relationships and a meaningful life, but only when one is operating out of clear, healthy self-interest.

Clear self-interest is difficult to discern when we live life at such cross-purposes with our deepest dreams and hopes that we no longer know who we truly are. Howard Thurman offers wisdom here: "At long last the only redemption from the paralysis of the cross-purpose is to seek with all possible intent to link one's deepest desire with one's choice of goal and to make of one's life a dedication to such an end."[1] We are most fulfilled, I think, when our deepest desire is linked to human need and the goal of the beloved community. The needs of the world are overwhelming and exhausting. I am not called to respond to every need, to every disaster, to every horror. I am not God. But God has placed within me an intuitive sense of when and where to engage in struggle. When what makes me come alive is joined to a particular world need, I have discovered a life-giving self-interest. The consequence is a deep sense of fulfillment and the joy of a life well lived.

---

1. Howard Thurman, *The Inward Journey* (Richmond, IN: Friends United, 1961), 75.

INNER HARMONY: *ST. GEORGE AND THE DRAGON*

When I become joyless, short-tempered, hypercritical, and pharisaical, it is probably time for me to step back from—and perhaps step out of—an issue campaign. And if others try to guilt-trip me into being part of their lockstep, dreary dutifulness, it's time for me to recall Emma Goldman's response to a young comrade who objected to her love of dancing and admonished her that it did not behoove an agitator to dance:

> I grew furious at the impudent interference of the boy. I told him to mind his own business. I was tired of having the Cause constantly thrown into my face. I did not believe that a Cause which stood for a beautiful ideal, for anarchism, for release and freedom from conventions and prejudice, should demand the denial of life and joy. I insisted that our Cause could not expect me to become a nun and that the movement should not be turned into a cloister. If it meant that, I did not want it. "I want freedom, the right to self-expression, everybody's right to beautiful, radiant things."[2]

A wise religious woman from Holy Wisdom Monastery in Madison, Wisconsin, once told me that the reason there are so few famous Benedictines in the world is that Benedictines live a balanced life. With a history of more than fifteen hundred years of communal practice in their tradition, many of the Benedictines have quite a bit to teach people like me about living fully alive and in harmony with self, society, nature, and God. Their foundational

---

2. Emma Goldman, *Living My Life* (New York: Knopf, 1934), 56.

text is the sixth-century *Rule of St. Benedict*, which is straightforward, practical, and realistic about human life and potential.

Here are a couple of instructions from the text that I find particularly delightful and down to earth. In chapter 22, St. Benedict writes that when they go to sleep at night, members of the community "should remove their knives, lest they accidentally cut themselves in their sleep."[3] In chapter 40, we get this advice: "It is, therefore, with some uneasiness that we specify the amount of food and drink for others. However, with due regard for the infirmities of the sick, we believe that a half bottle of wine a day is sufficient for each."[4]

In her profound exposition of the *Rule of St. Benedict*, Sr. Joan Chittister cautions about any notion of attaining spiritual perfection: "A visitor asked a monk, 'What do you do in the monastery?' The monastic replied, 'Well, we fall and we get up and we fall and we get up and we fall and we get up.'"[5] In the icon, the dragon is subdued rather than destroyed. And that assumes that you've got St. George riding in on a white horse.

Perhaps there is something inharmonious about beating oneself up because one is not attaining much inner harmony. The goal of spiritual perfection is self-defeating. It may well be that inner harmony has more to do with self-acceptance, warts and all, dragon and all. Sr. Chittister shares this story:

> The ancients say that once upon a time a disciple asked the elder, "Holy One, is there anything I can do to make myself Enlightened?"

---

3. Joan Chittister, *The Rule of Benedict* (New York: The Crossroad, 1993), 94.
4. Chittister, *Rule of Benedict*, 120.
5. Chittister, *Rule of Benedict*, 99–100.

And the Holy One answered, "As little as you can do to make the sun rise in the morning."

"Then of what use," the surprised disciple asked, "are the spiritual exercises you prescribe?"

"To make sure," the elder said, "that you are not asleep when the sun begins to rise."[6]

I recall visiting Dan Berrigan in New York a few years before his death. He was becoming physically fragile, but I remained in awe of Dan's centeredness during a lifetime of extraordinary activity. He was always alert to the present moment even as he wrote book after book of poetry and exposition of the Hebrew prophets; traveled constantly to lecture at universities, to lead retreats, and to speak about peacemaking; committed acts of civil disobedience and endured insolent judges and imprisonment; and gave selflessly to victims of AIDS, to those in hospice care, to homeless persons, to prisoners, to friends and family. Dan loved to tell jokes, cook a good meal for friends, drink with gusto, and swap stories. He took a long, observant walk every day. I've never met anyone with such inner wholeness amid a whirlwind of engagement in peace and justice ministry.

So I felt that Dan was the perfect person to answer a question that had been burdening me for a long time: "I don't feel like I'm making any spiritual progress. I feel stuck. Do you have any suggestions for me?"

Dan answered, "I gave up on those kinds of questions years ago. I'm just trying to live responsibly."

---

6. Chittister, *Rule of Benedict*, 32.

Dorothy Day (Gallery I)
11"x14" wood panel.
Egg tempera and gold leaf.

CHAPTER 11
Radical Personalism: *Dorothy Day*

The founder of the Catholic Worker Movement, Dorothy Day, is depicted in this icon in the kind of clothing one might pick up at a Salvation Army store. She lived her life among the poor and prayed, picketed, and organized against poverty and war. In her hand is a scroll—a sign that she was a prophetess who proclaimed the fierce word of God for justice and peace. Dorothy Day embodied, in the words of Dostoyevsky's Father Zossima, a "harsh and dreadful" love.[1]

In place of the usual rendering of the Greek word dikaiosuné as "righteousness," the picket sign in the *Dorothy Day* icon proclaims: "Blessed are those who hunger and thirst for justice." I think this is more faithful to the beatitude of Jesus and agitates against any pursuit of righteousness understood as a kind of individualized, pietistic, moral rectitude. Biblical righteousness is never separate from compassion and justice. The misinterpretation of the beatitude all too often forestalls justice and results not in righteousness

---

1. Fyodor Dostoyevsky, *The Brothers Karamazov*, trans. Constance Garnett (New York: Lowell Press, n.d.; Project Gutenberg, 2016), https://www.gutenberg.org/files/28054/28054-h/28054-h.html.

but in a sanctimonious illusion of holiness. Father Richard Rohr, OFM, has a similar view:

> This Beatitude is surely both spiritual and social. Most Bibles to this day soften this Beatitude: "hunger and thirst for what is right" or "for righteousness" are the more common faulty translations. But the word in Greek clearly means "justice." Notice that the concept of justice is used halfway through the Beatitudes and again at the very end. The couplet emphasizes an important point: To live a just life in this world is to identify with the longings and hungers of the poor, the meek, and those who weep.[2]

Rohr quotes a reflection on this beatitude by John Dear, a long-haul peace and justice activist:

> Righteousness is not just the private practice of doing good; it sums up the global responsibility of the human community to make sure every human being has what they need, that everyone pursues a fair sense of justice for every other human being, and that everyone lives in right relationship with one another, creation, and God. . . . Jesus instructs us to be passionate for social, economic, and racial justice. That's the real meaning of the Hebrew word for justice and the Jewish insistence on it. Resist systemic, structured, institutionalized injustice with every bone in your body, with all your might, with your very soul, he teaches. Seek justice as if it were your food and drink, your

---

2. Richard Rohr, "Blessed Are Those Who Hunger for Justice," Center for Action and Contemplation, February 2, 2018, https://cac.org/blessed-hunger-justice-2018-02-02/.

bread and water, as if it were a matter of life and death, which it is.³

I recall the decision of a large Assembly of God congregation in Milwaukee to end their short-lived membership in MICAH. Some members of this congregation became active in the education task force of MICAH and were part of a demonstration advocating at a state budget hearing for more funding of low-income schools. The protest was reported in an article in the *Milwaukee Journal Sentinel*, which featured a photograph of the demonstrators. The next week, the pastor and leaders of the congregation withdrew their membership from MICAH, righteously declaring that they were "a praying church." Indeed.

Dorothy Day embraced a radical personalism, which challenges all activists who are more interested in politics than people and all charitable people who ignore the need for systemic change. Central to her understanding of the gospel was the creation of community while working for justice with and among those at the bottom of society. In her own words:

> We cannot love God unless we love each other, and to love we must know each other. We know Him in the breaking of bread, and we know each other in the breaking of bread, and we are not alone anymore. Heaven is a banquet and life is a banquet, too, even with a crust, where there is companionship. We have all known the long loneliness

---

3. John Dear, *The Beatitudes of Peace: Meditations on the Beatitudes, Peacemaking and the Spiritual Life* (New London, CT: Twenty-Third Publications, 2016), 61–62.

and we have learned that the only solution is love and that love comes with community. It all happened while we sat there talking, and it is still going on.[4]

At its best, congregation-based organizing embodies the beloved community and is deeply committed to relationality. As Greg Galluzzo reminded me: "Issues are just an excuse for building relationships."

Dorothy Day was remarkable for her ability to work for justice on every level. Her radical personalism was lived out in compassionate service to the poor, in support of labor organizing, in defense of political prisoners, in direct actions for peace and justice both locally and globally, and in her prophetic opposition to what she called "this filthy rotten system." One of the limitations of congregation-based organizing is that its vision is all too often myopic. Constrained by an ideology that focuses almost exclusively on winnable issues and effectiveness in the public arena, such organizing rarely offers a prophetic word against the global imperialism of the United States, unrelenting warfare, or the voracious maw of the Pentagon.

I am reminded of Dr. Martin Luther King Jr.'s response when he was rebuked by some leaders of the civil rights movement who feared that his public opposition to the Vietnam War would weaken the struggle for civil rights:

> Cowardice asks the question, "Is it safe?" Expediency asks the question, "Is it politic?" Vanity asks the question, "Is it

---

4. Dorothy Day, *The Long Loneliness: An Autobiography* (New York: Harper & Row, 1952, 1981), 285–286.

popular?" But, conscience asks the question, "Is it right?" And there comes a time when one must take a position that is neither safe, nor politic, nor popular, but one must take it because one's conscience tells one that it is right.[5]

Spiritual wholeness is at stake when conscience is quieted for the sake of expediency or because it doesn't fit into an organizing frame. I am not suggesting that congregation-based organizing should turn activist. But I do think we have much to learn from Dorothy Day about conscience, about taking a resolute stand on burning issues, and, to paraphrase the prophet Habakkuk, about casting a vision so large and so plain that a runner may read it.

---

5. Martin Luther King Jr., "America's Chief Moral Dilemma" (1967, 1995). Speech delivered at the Hungry Club Forum, Atlanta, May 10, 1967.

Christ in Glory (Gallery J)
14"x22" wood panel.
Egg tempera and gold leaf.

CHAPTER 12
Final Hope: *Christ in Glory*

Then comes the end, when he hands over the kingdom to God the Father, after he has destroyed every ruler and every authority and power. For he must reign until he has put all his enemies under his feet. The last enemy to be destroyed is death. (1 Cor 15:24–26)

Then I looked, and I heard the voice of many angels surrounding the throne and the living creatures and the elders; they numbered myriads of myriads and thousands of thousands, singing with full voice, "Worthy is the Lamb that was slaughtered to receive power and wealth and wisdom and might and honor and glory and blessing!" Then I heard every creature in heaven and on earth and under the earth and in the sea, and all that is in them, singing, "To the one seated on the throne and to the Lamb be blessing and honor and glory and might forever and ever!" (Rev 5:11–13)

In this icon, *Christ in Glory*, Christ is surrounded by an oval mandorla and by two curved squares forming an octagonal star that symbolizes the future aeon. The inner square embraces only the figure of Christ in glory. This square is enclosed in the mandorla, which contains cherubim as representatives of the world of angels. In the corners of the outer square, which extend beyond the mandorla, are the symbols of the four evangelists: Matthew, a man; Mark, a lion; John, an eagle; and Luke, a bull.[1] The Greek letters in the halo proclaim Christ as the One Who Is, the I Am. The crucified, resurrected, and ascended Christ reigns in glory. The one who has overcome the world, demonic forces, principalities and powers, and even death itself now invites all the faithful into the fullness of the eschatological kingdom where God "will wipe every tear from their eyes. Death will be no more; mourning and crying and pain will be no more, for the first things have passed away" (Rev 21:4).

Amid the banalities, duplicities, horrors, betrayals, and degradations of human existence, Christians make the audacious claim that Christ has conquered evil and death, reigns in glory, will raise the dead on the Last Day, and will usher in an eternal kingdom of justice and peace. These claims were first made not during a time of triumphant Christendom when the seductions of imperial power, wealth, and conquest led to betrayal of the gospel of Jesus but during the days of the early church amidst vulnerability, frailty, and persecution. Ironically, the brightest hope is usually experienced by those who struggle in the deepest darkness.

Jim Wallis recalls a powerful example of such eschatological hope during the deep darkness of apartheid in South Africa. When the government tried to shut down opposition by canceling a political rally, Archbishop Desmond Tutu declared that he would

---

1. Leonid Ouspensky and Vladimir Lossky, *The Meaning of Icons* (Crestwood, NY: St. Vladimir's Seminary Press, 1983), 73.

hold an ecumenical worship service at St. George's Cathedral in Cape Town instead. Outside the cathedral, hundreds of South African security police, notorious for their violence, surrounded the cathedral, a show of force intended to intimidate and instill fear. As Tutu was preaching, police entered the cathedral and lined the walls. Weapons surrounded worshippers. But Archbishop Tutu was not intimidated. He preached against the evils of apartheid, declaring it could not endure. At one extraordinary point, he addressed the police directly: "You are powerful, very powerful . . . but I serve a God who cannot be mocked! . . . Since you have already lost, I invite you today to come and join the winning side!" The congregation's response was electric. Archbishop Tutu's bold challenge to tyranny transformed the band of worshippers. Their fear of the heavily armed security forces, who greatly outnumbered them, was replaced with determination and joy. The worshippers leaped to their feet, shouted praises of God, and began dancing. They danced out of the cathedral to meet the awaiting police and military forces of apartheid who, confounded by the fearless worshippers, backed up to provide space for the people to dance for freedom in the streets of Cape Town.[2]

My mood tends toward gloominess. I am easily discouraged. At low ebbs of urban ministry or organizing campaigns that were going nowhere, I have felt like a boxer in the early days of the "sport," when rounds were unlimited and the contest ended only when a boxer was knocked out or yielded. Emotionally, I felt knocked down over and over and over again. Each time I would

---

2. Paraphrasing Jim Wallis, *God's Politics* (San Francisco: Harper, 2005), 347–348. He quotes Archbishop Tutu in the book.

somehow get back on my feet. Beyond the precious encouragement of family and friends, what empowered me to stay in the struggle? Hope kept me going—a hope kindled and rekindled over the years by prayer, by the Eucharist, by the word, by the indwelling of the Spirit, by the community of faith, by the courage and example of a great cloud of witnesses that had gone before me and which surrounded me, and, ultimately, by a quiet trust in the eschatological victory of Christ that already is—and that most certainly is to come.

Physicists and philosophers contemplate the nature of time: its relativity, the possibility of its going in more than one direction, and whether it is simply an illusion. The icon of *Christ in Glory* suggests a strange view of time in which past, present, and future are interwoven. The present moment is infused with eschatological time, in which the past resurrection victory of Christ is at work now even as we anticipate the future eons. The reign of Christ is not limited by time or diminished by the current realities of evil, empire, and oppression. This is one way, I think, of understanding Wittgenstein's remark: "To believe in a God means to see that the facts of the world are not the end of the matter."[3]

As a parish pastor, one of my favorite feast days was All Saints. We would put sheets of paper on the walls of the sanctuary and write down the names of the faithful departed dear to the hearts of the congregants, interspersing them with names of some of the well-known peace and justice saints like Francis of Assisi, Sojourner Truth, Dietrich Bonhoeffer, Martin Luther King Jr., Oscar

---

3. Ludwig Wittgenstein, *Notebooks, 1914–1916* (New York: Harper Torchbooks, 1969), 74e.

Romero, and Dorothy Day. As bells tolled and we slowly read the names, I would always begin to enter the reality of the communion of saints who, while unseen, surround us and cheer us on.

We who struggle for peace and justice in this world are part of a continuum that long preceded us and that extends through the future into the eons to come. We may not feel like we accomplish much in our lifetimes. So often our victories in the public arena are offset by the next governor or mayor or the vicissitudes of life. And yet, what we do does matter. We learn what Dan Berrigan shared with me: "The results of our actions are in larger hands than our own." And we accept, with a certain modesty, the impermanence and limitations of our seeming successes.

Reinhold Niebuhr, reflecting on the irony of history, offered words of wisdom for those who find, despite long-haul struggle, that lasting victory remains elusive:

> Nothing that is worth doing can be achieved in our lifetime; therefore we must be saved by hope. Nothing which is true or beautiful or good makes complete sense in any immediate context of history; therefore we must be saved by faith. Nothing we do, however virtuous, can be accomplished alone; therefore we are saved by love. No virtuous act is quite as virtuous from the standpoint of our friend or foe as it is from our standpoint. Therefore we must be saved by the final form of love which is forgiveness.[4]

---

4. Reinhold Niebuhr, *The Irony of American History* (Chicago: University of Chicago Press, 1952, 2008), 63.

The icon *Christ in Glory* clears our spiritual glaucoma so that we can see that, in the end, justice and peace will prevail. For many this seems to be a pipe dream, but for those with the courage and spiritual stamina requisite for staying in the struggle, the truth of Dr. Martin Luther King Jr.'s vision rings true: "I believe that unarmed truth and unconditional love will have the final word in reality. This is why right, temporarily defeated, is stronger than evil triumphant."[5]

In the end, we will see that our ending is simply a beginning.

---

5. Martin Luther King Jr., Nobel Prize Acceptance Speech, Olso, Norway, December 10, 1964.

Practice

A Daily Office for Doing Justice

Introduction

While on sabbatical retreat at Christ in the Desert Monastery, deep in the remote Chama Canyon of New Mexico, I felt called to deepen my love of God through better-disciplined daily prayer. The Benedictine monks of Christ in the Desert Monastery pray together seven times daily, with lovely Gregorian chanting of the psalms and other biblical readings. (I confess that in this weeklong retreat, I arose only once for the 4:00 a.m. vigil. Showing up for lauds at 5:45 a.m. was more realistic for me. Also, I had the good sense to keep my off-key droning quietly to myself while the monks praised God with glorious chanting.)

I was there to connect with God on a deeper level and to seek more spiritual balance in my life, which had become frenetically imbalanced over the years. My daily demands as pastor of Incarnation Lutheran Church in Milwaukee and as director of the Gamaliel National Clergy Caucus, engaging in various organizing strategies locally and nationally, were fulfilling and meaningful but had begun to swallow up my soul. I sensed that I was increasingly anxious, testy, short with people, racing around, oblivious to my surroundings, quick to judgment—in short, running on empty. The gift of a sabbatical, graciously funded by the Lilly Foundation, made possible a privileged, four-month time of travel, rest, fun, and discernment. With my family, I visited the ancient monastic caves of Cappadocia in Turkey and remote monasteries in the mountains of Crete. Drawing on previous training in Byzantine iconography, I painted an icon, *Elijah in the Cave*, with egg tempera, ground pigments, and gold, and I meditatively entered the prophet's cave during that sacred process. Then, determined to go deeper into my soul and to seek some spiritual healing through wilderness solitude, I spent a week at Christ in the Desert Monastery.

At the monastery, I felt moved by the Spirit to fashion a Daily Office of readings and prayers, which could help me—and perhaps others—to deepen my love of God while organizing for a more just society. Although many worthy devotional aids and Daily Offices are in print, I have not yet found one that is sensitive to inclusive language, highlights the prophetic tradition of Scripture, and offers the kind of daily rhythm that goes to some depth while being realistically attentive to the time constraints of those engaged in active lives. Each selection of biblical passages and wisdom quotes will reveal a preference. Mine is clearly to connect with the great prophetic voices of Hebrew Scripture, with some of the central teachings and healings of Jesus, and with the wisdom of some who have faithfully struggled for justice and peace.

I offer this Daily Office as a resource for those seeking to find a more faithful balance in life: congregational core teams, leaders, organizers, and others who are struggling for a more just society, trying to love neighbor as self and desiring to love God with heart, soul, strength, and mind.

Acknowledgments

I want to thank Maureen Leach, OSF, and Nancy Schreck, OSF, for their gracious permission to use the psalms and the Magnificat from their book *Psalms Anew: In Inclusive Language*, originally published by Saint Mary's Press, Winona, Minnesota (1986), but now out of print.

For reasons that are made clear in "A Note on the Name of God" below, I have consistently preferred Yah instead of Yahweh for the sacred name of God in the psalms. I do so also with the permission of Sr. Leach and Sr. Schreck.

All Scripture quotations (other than the psalms and the Magnificat) are from the New Revised Standard Version Bible, copyright © 1989, National Council of the Churches of Christ in the United States of America.

In this text: *Yah* replaces Lord; *God* or *Who* replaces "Him" or "He" as points of divine reference. "Human One" replaces Son of Man; "One Who Reigns" replaces king. Occasional brackets indicate other wording preferred by me.

A Note on the Name of God

YHWH is an English approximation of the *Tetragrammaton*, the four aspirant consonants comprising the revealed name of God in the Hebrew Bible. We do not know with certainty how these four letters were pronounced, since they originally were without vowels. Some scholars have proposed *Yahweh*, but there is not full agreement on this pronunciation. YHWH probably derives from the Hebrew verb *hayah*, "to be," and thus we see the sacred name revealed to Moses at the burning bush translated as "I am who I am" or "I will be who I will be" (Exod 3:14; see also Exod 6:2–3). Other scholars propose different etymologies and translations. The uncertain pronunciation and translation of YHWH, the sacred name of God, is a reminder of the absolute transcendence of God, who is beyond the limitations of human language, thought, and imagination.

Yah is an ancient Hebrew name for God and may be a shortened form of YHWH. *Yah*, like YHWH, probably derives from the Hebrew *hayah*. Yah appears biblically as an interchangeable name for YHWH (Exod 15:2–3, Ps 118:14–15); in the evocative, two-word praise "Hallelu Yah" (Ps 150:1, 6); and as a significant constituent of names (Elijah, Jeremiah, Isaiah, Nehemiah). In some Jewish circles, the prohibition against vocalizing the *Tetragrammaton* (as early as the third century BCE) does not apply to Yah when that name is used in prayer and worship. For example, the Reform prayer book *Mishkan T'filah: A Reform Siddur* (New York: CCAR, 2007) transliterates the Hebrew in Psalm 150:6 as Hal'lu Yah while always shielding the *Holy Tetragrammaton* from pronunciation by having the congregation read *Adonai* instead.

English translations of the Bible generally use LORD to translate YHWH (see NRSV especially). This masculine, royal word obviously does not derive from YHWH. It translates "Adonai," which Jews pronounce in liturgy as a substitution for YHWH out of deep regard for the sacredness of the name of God.

My preference in this Daily Office is to use Yah where YHWH appears in the original Hebrew text. I also use Yah, instead of LORD, in several instances when Jesus is citing Hebrew Scripture where the original text has YHWH. Yah invites us to worship the God who transcends our language, our thought, and our tendencies to imagine God in masculine terms.

THE DAILY OFFICE

Week 1
Sunday • Morning Prayer

Versicle: God, open my lips.
Response: And my mouth shall proclaim your praise.

Glory be to God our Creator, to Jesus the Christ, and to the Holy Spirit who dwells in our midst, both now and forever. Amen.

Psalm 1

Oh, the joys of those who walk not after the advice of the wicked,
    nor stand in the path of sinners, nor sit in the seat of scoffers,
but delight in the law of Yah and ponder it day and night.
They are like trees planted by streams of water
that yield fruit in due season, whose leaves do not wither;
and everything they do prospers.
The ungodly are not so
but are like chaff which the wind blows away.
Therefore, they cannot stand firm when Judgment comes,
nor shall sinners find a place in the assembly of the righteous.

For God knows the way of the just,
but the way of the ungodly ends in ruin.

Quote

You want to do what is good, yet you move hastily, because you do not know you are moving in the wrong direction or that right beside you is a huge river of love flowing in one eternal direction. Stop your irrational movements, and jump into the river of love. It will carry you, and you will feel calm and free.—*Leo Tolstoy*

Genesis 1:3–4

Then God said, "Let there be light"; and there was light. And God saw that the light was good; and God separated the light from the darkness.

(Pause for silent reflection)

Prayer

Lord's Prayer*

May the light of God shine on all those who dwell in darkness and the shadow of death and guide my feet on the path of justice and peace. Amen.

> * As a regular or occasional alternative to the traditional Lord's Prayer, some may prefer this Prayer of Jesus composed by Parker Palmer:[1]

---

1. I first became aware of Parker Palmer's version of the Lord's Prayer about thirty years ago while on retreat at what is now called Holy

Heavenly Father, Heavenly Mother,
Holy and blessed is your true Name.
We pray for your reign of peace to come
We pray that your good will be done.
Let heaven and earth become one.
Give us this day the bread we need,
Give it to those who have none.
Let forgiveness flow like a river between us
From each one to each one to each one.
Lead us to holy innocence beyond the evil of our days.
Come swiftly, Mother, Father, come.
For yours is the power and the mercy and the glory.
Forever your Name is all in one. Amen.

Week 1
Sunday • Evening Prayer

V: O God of justice,
R: Come to my assistance.
V: O God of mercy,
R: Make haste to help me.
V: O God of love,
R: Grant me your peace.

Magnificat

My being proclaims your greatness,

Wisdom Monastery in Madison, Wisconsin. It can be found in *Peace Prayers*, edited by Carrie Leadingham, Joann E. Moschella, and Hilary M. Vartanian (San Francisco: Harper, 1992).

and my spirit finds joy in you, God my Savior.
For you have looked upon me, your servant, in my lowliness;
all ages to come shall call me blessed.
God, you who are mighty have done great things for me.
Holy is your name.
Your mercy is from age to age toward those who fear you.
You have shown might with your arm and confused the proud in their inmost thoughts.
You have deposed the mighty from their thrones
and raised the lowly to high places.
The hungry you have given every good thing
while the rich you have sent away empty.
You have upheld Israel your servant, ever mindful of your mercy
even as you promised our ancestors;
promised Abraham, Sarah, and their descendants forever.

Matthew 4:8–10

Again, the devil took [Jesus] to a very high mountain and showed him all the kingdoms of the world and their splendor; and he said to him, "All these I will give you, if you will fall down and worship me." Jesus said to him, "Away with you, Satan! for it is written, 'Worship Yah your God, and serve only Yah.'"

(Pause for silent reflection)

Prayer

Lord's Prayer (or alternative)

May we find our rest in you, O God, both now and at the end of life's journey. Amen.

Week 1
Monday • Morning Prayer

V: O God, come to my assistance.
R: O Christ, make haste to help me.
V: O Sophia, guide my path this day.
R: Blessed Trinity, draw me toward you.

Psalm 2

Why this tumult among nations,
among peoples this useless murmuring?
The rulers of the earth arise
and plot against Yah and the Anointed.
"Come, let us break their chains!
Come, let us cast off their yoke!"
The One who sits in the heavens laughs;
Yah derides them.
Then God will speak to them in anger
And in rage will strike them with terror.
"It is I who have set up my ruler on Zion, my holy mountain."
I will proclaim the decree of God.
God said to me: "You are mine.
It is I who have begotten you this day.
Ask and I shall bequeath you the nations,
make the ends of the earth in your possession.
With a rod of iron you will break them,
shatter them like a potter's jar."
Now, O leaders, understand;
take warning, rulers of the earth.
Serve God with awe and trembling, paying homage,
lest God be angry and you perish;

for God's anger will suddenly blaze.
Blessed are they who put their trust in God.

Quote

Do not shun power nor despise it. But use it correctly. When is power used correctly? Power is made for service. I am your servant; I am not your master. Be a servant. Not a master.—*Mechtild of Magdeburg*

Exodus 3:7–8a, 9–11

Then God said, "I have observed the misery of my people who are in Egypt; I have heard their cry on account of their taskmasters. Indeed, I know their sufferings, and I have come down to deliver them from the Egyptians, and to bring them up out of that land to a good and broad land, a land flowing with milk and honey. . . . The cry of the Israelites has now come to me; I have also seen how the Egyptians oppress them. So come, I will send you to Pharaoh to bring my people, the Israelites, out of Egypt." But Moses said to God, "Who am I that I should go out to Pharaoh, and bring the Israelites out of Egypt?"

(Pause for silent reflection)

Prayer

Lord's Prayer (or alternative)

May the light of God shine on all those who dwell in darkness and the shadow of death and guide my feet on the path of justice and peace. Amen.

Week 1
Monday • Evening Prayer

V: O God of justice,
R: Come to my assistance.
V: O God of mercy,
R: Make haste to help me.
V: O God of love,
R: Grant me your peace.

Psalm 63:1–8

O God, you are my God whom I eagerly seek;
for you my flesh longs and my soul thirsts
like the earth, parched, lifeless, and without water.
I have gazed toward you in the sanctuary
to see your power and your glory.
For your love is better than life;
my lips shall glorify you.
Thus will I praise you while I live;
lifting up my hands, I will call upon your name.
As with the riches of a banquet shall my soul be filled,
and with exultant lips my mouth shall praise you.
On my bed I will remember you,
and through the night watches I will meditate on you:
because you are my help,
and in the shadow of your wings I shout for joy.
My soul clings to you;
your right hand upholds me.

Matthew 5:2-12

Then [Jesus] began to speak, and taught them, saying:
"Blessed are the poor in spirit, for theirs is the kingdom of heaven.
Blessed are those who mourn, for they will be comforted.
Blessed are the meek, for they will inherit the earth.
Blessed are those who hunger and thirst for righteousness, for they will be filled.
Blessed are the merciful, for they will receive mercy.
Blessed are the pure in heart, for they will see God.
Blessed are the peacemakers, for they will be called children of God.
Blessed are those who are persecuted for righteousness' sake, for theirs is the kingdom of heaven.
Blessed are you when people revile you and persecute you and utter all kinds of evil against you falsely on my account. Rejoice and be glad, for your reward is great in heaven, for in the same way they persecuted the prophets who were before you."

(Pause for silent reflection)

Prayer

Lord's Prayer (or alternative)

May we find our rest in you, O God, both now and at the end of life's journey. Amen.

Week 1
Tuesday • Morning Prayer

V: Weaver of worlds, seen and unseen,
R: Weaver of light and darkness, weal and woe,

V: Weaver of the warp and weft of history,
R: Weave my life into the fabric of your will.

Psalm 8

O God, our God, how glorious is your name over all the earth!
Your glory is praised in the heavens.
Out of the mouths of children and babes
you have fashioned praise because of your foes,
to silence the enemy and the rebellious.
When I look at your heavens, the work of your hands,
the moon and the stars which you created—
who are we that you should be mindful of us,
that you should care for us?
You have made us little less than the gods
and crowned us with glory and honor.
You have given us rule over the works of your hands,
putting all things under our feet:
all sheep and oxen, yes, and the beasts of the field;
the birds of the air, the fishes of the sea,
and whatever swims the paths of the seas.
God, our God, how glorious is your name over all the earth!

Quote

The day of my spiritual awakening was the day I saw and knew I saw all things in God and God in all things.—*Mechtild of Magdeburg*

Genesis 28:16-17

Then Jacob woke from his sleep and said, "Surely Yah is in this place and I did not know it!" And he was afraid, and said, "How awesome is this place! This is none other than the house of God, and this is the gate of heaven."

(Pause for silent reflection)

Prayer

Lord's Prayer (or alternative)

May the light of God shine on all those who dwell in darkness and the shadow of death and guide my feet on the path of justice and peace. Amen.

Week 1
Tuesday • Evening Prayer

V: O God of justice,
R: Come to my assistance.
V: O God of mercy,
R: Make haste to help me.
V: O God of love,
R: Grant me your peace.

Psalm 10:1-6, 9-12

Why do you stand aloof, O God?
Why do you hide yourself in times of trouble?
In arrogance the wicked oppress the poor

who are caught in the schemes that the wicked have devised.
For the wicked boast of their heart's desires,
and those greedy for gain curse and renounce you.
The wicked do not seek you, because of their pride;
all their thoughts are, "There is no God."
The ways of the wicked prosper at all times;
your judgments are on high, out of their sight.
As for all their foes, they scorn them.
They think in their hearts, "We shall not be moved;
throughout all generations we shall not meet adversity."
They lie in wait that they may seize the poor;
they catch the afflicted and draw them into their net.
The helpless are crushed, sink down, and fall by their might.
They think in their hearts,
"God forgets, hides, and never will see it."
Arise, Yah! O God, lift up your hand!
Forget not the afflicted!

Matthew 5:21–24

You have heard that it was said to those of ancient times, "You shall not murder"; and "whoever murders shall be liable to judgment." But I say to you that if you are angry with a brother or sister, you will be liable to judgment; and if you insult a brother or sister, you will be liable to the council; and if you say, "You fool," you will be liable to the hell of fire. So when you are offering your gift at the altar, if you remember that your brother or sister has something against you, leave your gift there before the altar and go; first be reconciled to your brother or sister, and then come and offer your gift.

(Pause for silent reflection)

Prayer

Lord's Prayer (or alternative)

May we find our rest in you, O God, both now and at the end of life's journey. Amen.

Week 1
Wednesday • Morning Prayer

V: O Sacred Source of all light,
R: Enlighten my darkness.
V: O God who dwells in uncreated light,
R: In your light, I see light.

Psalm 42:1–5

Like the deer that yearns for running streams,
so my soul is yearning for you, my God.
My soul is thirsting for God, the living God.
When can I enter to see the face of God?
My tears have become my food night and day,
and I hear it said all day long: "Where is your God?"
I will remember all these things as I pour out my soul:
how I would lead the joyous procession into the house of God,
with cries of gladness and thanksgiving,
the multitude wildly happy.
Why are you so sad, my soul?
Why sigh within me?
Hope in God;
for I will yet praise my savior and my God.

Quote

Worship is a way of seeing the world in the light of God.
—*Abraham Joshua Heschel*

Exodus 15:20–21

Then the prophet Miriam, Aaron's sister, took a tambourine in her hand; and all the women went out after her with tambourines and with dancing. And Miriam sang to them: "Sing to Yah, [who] has triumphed gloriously; horse and rider Yah has thrown into the sea."

(Pause for silent reflection)

Prayer

Lord's Prayer (or alternative)

May the light of God shine on all those who dwell in darkness and the shadow of death and guide my feet on the path of justice and peace. Amen.

Week 1
Wednesday • Evening Prayer

V: O God of justice,
R: Come to my assistance.
V: O God of mercy,
R: Make haste to help me.
V: O God of love,
R: Grant me your peace.

Psalm 36

Sin speaks to sinners in the depths of their hearts.
No awe of God is before their eyes.
They so flatter themselves that they do not know their guilt.
In their mouths are lies and foolishness. Gone is all wisdom.
They plot the downfall of goodness as they lie on their beds.
They set their feet on evil ways; they hold to what is evil.
Your love, Yah, reaches to heaven;
your faithfulness to the skies.
Your justice is like a mountain—your judgments like the deep.
To all creation you give protection.
Your people find refuge in the shelter of your wings.
They feast on the riches of your house;
they drink from the stream of your delight.
You are the source of life,
and in your light we see light.
Continue your love to those who know you,
doing justice to the upright in heart.
Let the foot of the proud not crush me,
nor the hand of the wicked drive me away.
See how the evildoers have fallen!
Flung down, they shall never rise.

Matthew 5:38–39, 43–44

You have heard that it was said, "An eye for an eye and a tooth for a tooth." But I say to you, Do not [violently] resist an evildoer. But if anyone strikes you on the right cheek, turn the other also; . . . You have heard that it was said, "You shall love your neighbor and hate your enemy." But I say to you, Love your enemies and pray for those who persecute you.

(Pause for silent reflection)

Prayer

Lord's Prayer (or alternative)

May we find our rest in you, O God, both now and at the end of life's journey. Amen.

Week 1
Thursday • Morning Prayer

V: All-powerful God,
R: Grant me wisdom to do your will today.
V: All-merciful God,
R: Fill my heart with compassion.
V: All-loving God,
R: Enflame my soul with love of you.

Psalm 15

Yah, who has the right to enter your tent,
or to live on your holy mountain?
Those whose way of life is blameless,
who always do what is right, who speak the truth from their heart,
whose tongue is not used for slander,
who do no wrong to friends, cast no discredit on neighbors,
who look with contempt on the reprobate,

but honor those who fear you,
who stand by a pledge at all cost,
who do not ask interest on loans,
and cannot be bribed to exploit the innocent.
If they do all this, nothing can ever shake them.

Quote

Don't ask what the world needs. Ask what makes you come alive, and go do it. Because what the world needs is people who have come alive.—*Howard Thurman*

Leviticus 19:33–34

When an alien resides with you in your land, you shall not oppress the alien. The alien who resides with you shall be to you as the citizen among you; you shall love the alien as yourself, for you were aliens in the land of Egypt: I am Yah your God.

(Pause for silent reflection)

Prayer

Lord's Prayer (or alternative)

May the light of God shine on all those who dwell in darkness and the shadow of death and guide my feet on the path of justice and peace. Amen.

Week 1
Thursday • Evening Prayer

V: O God of justice,
R: Come to my assistance.
V: O God of mercy,
R: Make haste to help me.
V: O God of love,
R: Grant me your peace.

Psalm 53

The fools say in their hearts, "There is no God."
They are corrupt, and their ways are evil.
There are none who do good.
God looks down from heaven
to see if there are any that are wise, any who seek after God.
Everyone has fallen away; they are all alike—corrupt.
There are none that do good—no, not even one.
Have these evildoers no understanding—
those who eat up my people as they eat bread
and do not call upon God?
There they are, overwhelmed with fear,
in fear whose source is unknown!
For God will scatter the bones of evildoers;
they will be put to shame, for God has rejected them.
Oh, that deliverance for Israel would come to Zion!
When God restores the well-being of faithful people,
then Jacob will rejoice and Israel be glad.

Matthew 7:1–3

Do not judge, so that you may not be judged. For with the judgment you make you will be judged, and the measure you give will be the measure you get. Why do you see the speck in your neighbor's eye, but do not notice the log in your own eye?

(Pause for silent reflection)

Prayer

Lord's Prayer (or alternative)

May we find our rest in you, O God, both now and at the end of life's journey. Amen.

Week 1
Friday • Morning Prayer

V: I sing as I arise today.
R: I call on my Creator's might:
V: the will of God to be my guide,
R: the eye of God to be my sight,
V: the word of God to be my speech,
R: the hand of God to be my stay,
V: the shield of God to be my strength,
R: the path of God to be my way. Amen.

—*based on St. Patrick's "Breastplate"*

Psalm 51:1-14

In your goodness, O God, have mercy on me;
with gentleness wipe away my faults.
Cleanse me of guilt; free me from my sins.
My faults are always before me; my sins haunt my mind.
I have sinned against you and no other—
knowing that my actions were wrong in your eyes.
Your judgment is what I deserve;
your sentence supremely fair.
As you know I was born in guilt,
from conception a sinner at heart.
But you love true sincerity,
so you teach me the depths of wisdom.
Until I am clean, bathe me with hyssop;
wash me until I am whiter than snow.
Infuse me with joy and gladness;
Let these bones you have crushed dance for joy.
Please do not stare at my sins; blot out all my guilt.
Create a pure heart in me, O my God;
renew me with a steadfast spirit.
Don't drive me away from your presence,
or take your Holy Spirit from me.
Once more be my savior; revive my joy.
Strengthen and sharpen my still weak spirit.
And I will teach transgressors your ways;
then sinners will return to you, too.
Release me from death, God my Savior,
and I will announce your justice.

Quote

I believe that unarmed truth and unconditional love will have the final word in reality. This is why right, temporarily defeated, is stronger than evil triumphant.—*Martin Luther King Jr.*

Deuteronomy 30:19

I call heaven and earth to witness against you today that I have set before you life and death, blessings and curses. Choose life so that you and your descendants may live.

(Pause for silent reflection)

Prayer

Lord's Prayer (or alternative)

May the light of God shine on all those who dwell in darkness and the shadow of death and guide my feet on the path of justice and peace. Amen.

Week 1
Friday • Evening Prayer

V: O God of justice,
R: Come to my assistance.
V: O God of mercy,
R: Make haste to help me.
V: O God of love,
R: Grant me your peace.

Psalm 86:1-11

Listen to me, O God, and answer me,
because I am poor and afflicted.
Save me from death, because I am loyal to you;
save me, because I am your servant and trust in you.
You are my God, so be merciful to me.
I call to you all day long.
Make your servant glad, because I lift my soul to you.
Yah, you are good and forgiving,
full of faithful love for all who pray to you.
Listen to my prayer; hear my cry for help.
I call to you in times of trouble,
for you answer my prayer.
There is no other god like you, Yah—
not one who can do the deeds you do.
All the nations you have created will come and worship you.
They will praise your greatness
because only you, God, are mighty; only you do wonderful deeds.
Teach me your way, Yah, and I will obey you faithfully;
give me an undivided heart that I may fear your name.

Mark 5:25-29

Now there was a woman who had been suffering from hemorrhages for twelve years. She had endured much under many physicians and had spent all that she had; and she was no better but rather grew worse. She had heard about Jesus, and she came up behind him in the crowd and touched his cloak, for she said, "If I but touch his clothes, I will be made well." Immediately her hemorrhage stopped; and she felt in her body that she was healed of her disease.

(Pause for silent reflection)

Prayer

Lord's Prayer (or alternative)

May we find our rest in you, O God, both now and at the end of life's journey. Amen.

Week 1
Saturday • Morning Prayer

V: Creator of all that is, seen and unseen,
R: Praise to you! Create me anew this day.
V: Savior and Redeemer of the world,
R: Praise to you! Free me from all bondage and oppression.
V: Spirit of life now and eternal,
R: Praise to you! Show me the path I must walk today.

Psalm 84

How I love your dwelling place, Yah Sabaoth!
How my soul yearns and pines for your courts!
My heart and my flesh cry out to you, the living God.
Finally, the sparrow has found its home,
the swallow a nest for its young—
your altars, Yah Sabaoth, O my God.
Happy those who dwell in your house
and praise you all day long.

Happy those whose strength is in you;
they have courage to make the pilgrimage!
As they go through the Valley of the Weeper,
they make it a place of springs,
clothed in generous growth by early rains.
They make their way from strength to strength,
soon to see God in Zion.
Yah Sabaoth, hear my prayer;
listen, God of Jacob and Rebekah.
Now look on us, God our Shield, and be kind to your anointed.
Only one day in your courts
is worth more than a thousand elsewhere;
merely to stand at the door of God's house
is better than living with the wicked.
For you, God, are a sun and shield, bestowing grace and glory.
Yah withholds nothing good
from those who walk without blame.
Yah Sabaoth, happy are those who put their trust in you.

Quote

Christianity without discipleship is always Christianity without Christ.—*Dietrich Bonhoeffer*

Ruth 1:15-17

So [Naomi] said, "See, your sister-in-law has gone back to her people and to her gods; return after your sister-in-law." But Ruth said, "Do not press me to leave you or to turn back from following you! Where you go, I will go; where you lodge, I will lodge; your people shall be my people, and your God my God. Where you die,

I will die—there will I be buried. May Yah do thus and so to me, and more as well, if even death parts me from you!"

(Pause for silent reflection)

Prayer

Lord's Prayer (or alternative)

May the light of God shine on all those who dwell in darkness and the shadow of death and guide my feet on the path of justice and peace. Amen.

Week 1
Saturday • Evening Prayer

V: O God of justice,
R: Come to my assistance.
V: O God of mercy,
R: Make haste to help me.
V: O God of love,
R: Grant me your peace.

Psalm 56:1–11a

Be gracious to me, O God, for the enemy persecutes me;
my adversaries harass me all day long.
All day long my watchful foes persecute me;
countless are those who oppress me.
Appear on high in my day of fear. I put my trust in you.
With God to help me I will stand firm.

In God I trust, and I shall not be afraid.
What can mortals do to me?
All day long they plot to harm me: all their thoughts are hostile.
They are on the lookout; they conspire and spy on my footsteps.
But while they lie in wait for me, it is they who will not escape.
O God, in your anger bring ruin on the nations.
Enter my lament in your book; store every tear in your flask.
Then my enemies will be turned back
on the day when I call upon you;
for this I know—that God is with me.
In God I trust and shall not be afraid.

Mark 4:35–41

On that day, when evening had come, [Jesus] said to them, "Let us go across to the other side." And leaving the crowd behind, they took him with them in the boat, just as he was. Other boats were with him. A great windstorm arose, and the waves beat into the boat, so that the boat was already being swamped. But he was in the stern, asleep on the cushion; and they woke him up and said to him, "Teacher, do you not care that we are perishing?" He woke up and rebuked the wind, and said to the sea, "Peace! Be still!" Then the wind ceased, and there was a dead calm. He said to them, "Why are you afraid? Have you still no faith?" And they were filled with great awe and said to one another, "Who then is this, that even the wind and the sea obey him?"

(Pause for silent reflection)

Prayer

Lord's Prayer (or alternative)

May we find our rest in you, O God, both now and at the end of life's journey. Amen.

Week 2
Sunday • Morning Prayer

Versicle: God, open my lips.
Response: And my mouth shall proclaim your praise.

Glory be to God our Creator, to Jesus the Christ, and to the Holy Spirit who dwells in our midst, both now and forever. Amen.

Psalm 27:1–6

God, you are my light and my salvation; whom shall I fear?
You are the stronghold of my life; of whom shall I be afraid?
When evildoers assail me, uttering slanders against me,
my adversaries and foes, they shall stumble and fall.
Though a host encamp against me, my heart will not fear;
though war arise against me, yet I will be confident.
One thing I have asked of you, Yah, this I seek:
to dwell in your house all the days of my life,
to behold your beauty and to contemplate on your Temple.
For you will hide me in your shelter in the day of trouble,
you will conceal me under the cover of your tent
and will set me high upon a rock.
And now my head shall be lifted up
above my enemies on every side.
I will offer in your tent sacrifices with shouts of joy;
I will sing and make melody to you.

Quote

Religion without humanity is a poor human stuff.—*Sojourner Truth*

1 Samuel 3:8–10

Yah called Samuel again, a third time. And he got up and went to Eli, and said, "Here I am, for you called me." Then Eli perceived that Yah was calling the boy. Therefore Eli said to Samuel, "Go, lie down; and if Yah calls you, you shall say, 'Speak, Yah, for your servant is listening.'" So Samuel went and lay down in his place. Now Yah came and stood there, calling as before, "Samuel! Samuel!" And Samuel said, "Speak, for your servant is listening."

(Pause for silent reflection)

Prayer

Lord's Prayer (or alternative)

Gracious God, grant me strength, wisdom, and courage to do justice, to love kindness, and to walk humbly with you today.

Week 2
Sunday • Evening Prayer

V: O God, lead me to your still waters.
R: Restore my soul.
V: Lead me in right paths.
R: Guide me through the darkest valley.

Magnificat

My being proclaims your greatness,
and my spirit finds joy in you, God my Savior.
For you have looked upon me, your servant, in my lowliness;
all ages to come shall call me blessed.
God, you who are mighty have done great things for me.
Holy is your name.
Your mercy is from age to age toward those who fear you.
You have shown might with your arm and confused the proud in their inmost thoughts.
You have deposed the mighty from their thrones
and raised the lowly to high places.
The hungry you have given every good thing
while the rich you have sent away empty.
You have upheld Israel your servant, ever mindful of your mercy even as you promised our ancestors;
promised Abraham, Sarah, and their descendants forever.

Mark 12:28–31

One of the scribes came near and heard them disputing with one another, and seeing that he answered them well, he asked him, "Which commandment is the first of all?" Jesus answered, "The first is, 'Hear O Israel: Yah our God, Yah is one; you shall love Yah your God with all your heart, and with all your soul, and with all your mind, and with all your strength.' The second is this, 'You shall love your neighbor as yourself.' There is no other commandment greater than these."

(Pause for silent reflection)

Prayer

Lord's Prayer (or alternative)

As the evening shadows come, O God, protect all those dear to my heart, and draw me ever closer to you. Amen.

Week 2
Monday • Morning Prayer

V: O God, come to my assistance.
R: O Christ, make haste to help me.
V: O Sophia, guide my path this day.
R: Blessed Trinity, draw me toward you.

Psalm 82

God arises in the divine assembly
and judges in the midst of the gods:
"How long will you defend the unjust
and favor the cause of the wicked?"
Defend the poor and the orphaned;
render justice to the afflicted and the oppressed.
Rescue the lowly and the poor;
from the clutches of the wicked deliver them.
They have neither knowledge nor understanding—
they walk about blindly.
All the order of the world is shaken.
I said: "You are gods, all of you.
Yet like mortals you shall die—fall like any ruler."
Rise, O God; judge the earth,
for yours are all the nations.

Quote

We have assumed the name of peacemakers, but we have been, by and large, unwilling to pay any significant price. And because we want the peace with half a heart and half a life and will, the war, of course, continues, because the waging of war, by its nature, is total—but the waging of peace, by our own cowardice, is partial.—*Daniel Berrigan*

2 Chronicles 7:14

If my people who are called by my name humble themselves, pray, seek my face, and turn from their wicked ways, then I will hear from heaven, and will forgive their sin and heal their land.

(Pause for silent reflection)

Prayer

Lord's Prayer (or alternative)

Gracious God, grant me strength, wisdom, and courage to do justice, to love kindness, and to walk humbly with you today.

Week 2
Monday • Evening Prayer

V: O God, lead me to your still waters.
R: Restore my soul.
V: Lead me in right paths.
R: Guide me through the darkest valley.

Psalm 3:1–5

Yah, more and more people are turning against me,
more and more rebelling against me,
more and more saying about me,
"There is no help for you in your God."
But you, Yah, my encircling shield,
my glory, you help me lift up my head.
Loudly I cry to Yah,
who answers me from the holy mountain.
Now I can lie down and sleep
and then awake, for Yah sustains me.

Matthew 5:14–16

You are the light of the world. A city built on a hill cannot be hid. No one after lighting a lamp puts it under the bushel basket, but on the lampstand, and it gives light to all in the house. In the same way, let your light shine before others, so that they may see your good works and give glory to your Father in heaven.

(Pause for silent reflection)

Prayer

Lord's Prayer (or alternative)

As the evening shadows come, O God, protect all those dear to my heart, and draw me ever closer to you. Amen.

Week 2
Tuesday • Morning Prayer

V: Weaver of worlds, seen and unseen,
R: Weaver of light and darkness, weal and woe,
V: Weaver of the warp and weft of history,
R: Weave my life into the fabric of your will.

Psalm 62

For God alone my soul waits. My help comes from God,
who alone is my rock, my stronghold, my fortress: I stand firm.
How long will you all attack me to break me down
as though I were a tottering wall or a sagging fence?
Their plan is only to destroy. They take pleasure in lies.
With their mouths they utter blessing,
but in their hearts they curse.
For God alone my soul waits; for my hope comes from God, who
    alone is my rock, my stronghold, my fortress. I stand firm.
In God is my salvation and glory, the rock of my strength.
All you people, take refuge in God. Trusting at all times,
pour out your hearts before God, our Refuge.
Common folk are only a breath; those of rank, an illusion.
Placed in the scales, they rise; they weigh less than a breath.
Do not put your trust in oppression
nor in vain hopes or plunder.
Do not set your heart on riches even when they abound.
For God has declared only one thing; only two do I know:
that to God alone belongs power;
and that you, Yah, are steadfast love.
Surely you repay all according to their deeds.

Quote

It is possible to become discouraged about the injustice we see everywhere. But God did not promise us that the world would be humane and just. God gives us the gift of life and allows us to choose the way we will use our limited time on earth. It is an awesome opportunity.—*Cesar Chavez*

Proverbs 8:1–5, 10–11, 35–36

Does not wisdom call, and does not understanding raise her voice? On the heights, beside the way, at the crossroads she takes her stand; beside the gates in front of the town, at the entrance of the portals she cries out: "To you, O people, I call, and my cry is to all that live. O simple ones, learn prudence; acquire intelligence, you who lack it. . . . Take my instruction instead of silver, and knowledge rather than choice gold; for wisdom is better than jewels, and all that you may desire cannot compare with her. . . . For whoever finds me finds life and obtains favor from Yah; but those who miss me injure themselves; all who hate me love death."

(Pause for silent reflection)

Prayer

Lord's Prayer (or alternative)

Gracious God, grant me strength, wisdom, and courage to do justice, to love kindness, and to walk humbly with you today.

Week 2
Tuesday • Evening Prayer

V: O God, lead me to your still waters.
R: Restore my soul.
V: Lead me in right paths.
R: Guide me through the darkest valley.

Psalm 123

To you have I lifted up my eyes, you who dwell in the heavens.
Behold, like the eyes of slaves are on the hand of their master,
like the eyes of servants on the hand of their mistress,
so are our eyes on you, Yah our God,
till you show us your mercy.
Have mercy on us, Yah! Have mercy!
We have endured much contempt.
Indeed, all too full is our soul
with scorn from the rich,
with scorn from the proud.

Mark 8:34–36

[Jesus] called the crowd with his disciples, and said to them, "If any want to become my followers, let them deny themselves and take up their cross and follow me. For those who want to save their life will lose it, and those who lose their life for my sake, and for the sake of the gospel, will save it. For what will it profit them to gain the whole world and forfeit their life?"

(Pause for silent reflection)

Prayer

Lord's Prayer (or alternative)

As the evening shadows come, O God, protect all those dear to my heart, and draw me ever closer to you. Amen.

Week 2
Wednesday • Morning Prayer

V: O Sacred Source of all light,
R: Enlighten my darkness.
V: O God who dwells in uncreated light,
R: In your light, I see light.

Psalm 120

When I was in trouble I called to you, Yah,
and you answered me.
Save me from liars and deceivers!
You liars, what will God do to you? How will God punish you?
With a soldier's sharp arrows, with burning coals!
Living among you is as bad as living in Meshech
or among the people of Kedar!
Too long have I lived with people who hate peace!
When I speak of peace,
they are for war.

Quote

If you are neutral in situations of injustice, you have chosen the side of the oppressor. If an elephant has its foot on the tail of a mouse and you say that you are neutral, the mouse will not appreciate your neutrality.—*Archbishop Desmond Tutu*

Isaiah 2:4

Yah shall judge between the nations
and shall arbitrate for many peoples;
they shall beat their swords into plowshares
and their spears into pruning hooks;
nation shall not lift up sword against nation,
neither shall they learn war any more.

(Pause for silent reflection)

Prayer

Lord's Prayer (or alternative)

Gracious God, grant me strength, wisdom, and courage to do justice, to love kindness, and to walk humbly with you today.

Week 2
Wednesday • Evening Prayer

V: O God, lead me to your still waters.
R: Restore my soul.
V: Lead me in right paths.
R: Guide me through the darkest valley.

Psalm 126

When God brought back the captives of Zion,
we were like those who dream.
Then our mouths were filled with laughter
and our tongues with rejoicing;
then they said among the nations,
"Yah has done great things for them."
Yah has done great things for us; we are truly glad.
Restore our fortunes, Yah, like the streams in the Negeb!
May those who sow in tears reap with songs of joy!
Those that go forth weeping, carrying the seed for sowing,
shall come home with shouts of joy,
bringing the sheaves with them.

Mark 9:33–37

Then they came to Capernaum; and when [Jesus] was in the house he asked them, "What were you arguing about on the way?" But they were silent, for on the way they had argued with one another who was the greatest. He sat down, called the twelve, and said to them, "Whoever wants to be first must be last of all and servant of all." Then he took a little child and put it among them; and taking it in his arms, he said to them, "Whoever welcomes one such child in my name welcomes me, and whoever welcomes me welcomes not me but the one who sent me."

(Pause for silent reflection)

Prayer

Lord's Prayer (or alternative)

As the evening shadows come, O God, protect all those dear to my heart, and draw me ever closer to you. Amen.

Week 2
Thursday • Morning Prayer

V: All-powerful God,
R: Grant me wisdom to do your will today.
V: All-merciful God,
R: Fill my heart with compassion.
V: All-loving God,
R: Enflame my soul with love of you.

Psalm 12

Help, O Yah! for no one now is devout;
faithfulness has vanished from among the people.
People speak falsehood to their neighbor;
with smooth lips and double heart they speak.
May Yah destroy all smooth lips, every boastful tongue—
those who say, "We are strong with our tongues;
our lips are our own. Who rules over us?"
"Because they rob the afflicted, and the needy sigh,
now will I arise," says Yah;
"I will grant safety to those who long for it."
The promises of Yah are sure,
like tried silver, freed from dross, sevenfold refined.
You will guard us and preserve us always

from this generation,
while about us the wicked strut,
and in high places are the basest of people.

Quote

Walk the street with us into history. Get off the sidewalk.—
Dolores Huerta

Isaiah 6:6–8

Then one of the seraphs flew to me, holding a live coal that had been taken from the altar with a pair of tongs. The seraph touched my mouth with it and said: "Now that this has touched your lips, your guilt has departed and your sin is blotted out." Then I heard the voice of God saying, "Whom shall I send, and who will go for us?" And I said, "Here am I; send me!"

(Pause for silent reflection)

Prayer

Lord's Prayer (or alternative)

Gracious God, grant me strength, wisdom, and courage to do justice, to love kindness, and to walk humbly with you today.

Week 2
Thursday • Evening Prayer

V: O God, lead me to your still waters.
R: Restore my soul.

V: Lead me in right paths.
R: Guide me through the darkest valley.

Psalm 139:1–14

Yah, you search me and know me.
You know if I am standing or sitting.
You perceive my thoughts from far away.
Whether I walk or lie down, you are watching;
you are familiar with all my ways.
Before a word is even on my tongue, Yah,
you know it completely.
Close behind and close in front you hem me in,
shielding me with your hand.
Such knowledge is beyond my understanding,
too high beyond my reach.
Where could I go to escape your spirit?
Where could I flee from your presence?
If I climb to the heavens, you are there;
there, too, if I sink to Sheol.
If I flew to the point of sunrise—or far across the sea—
your hand would still be guiding me,
your right hand holding me.
If I asked darkness to cover me
and light to become night around me,
that darkness would not be dark to you;
night would shine as the day.
You created my inmost being
and knit me together in my mother's womb.
For all these mysteries—for the wonder of myself,
for the wonder of your works—
I thank you.

Mark 10: 17–22

As [Jesus] was setting out on a journey, a man ran up and knelt before him, and asked him, "Good Teacher, what must I do to inherit eternal life?" Jesus said to him, "Why do you call me good? No one is good but God alone. You know the commandments: 'You shall not murder; You shall not commit adultery; You shall not steal; You shall not bear false witness; You shall not defraud; Honor your father and your mother.'" He said to him, "Teacher, I have kept all these since my youth." Jesus, looking at him, loved him and said, "You lack one thing; go, sell what you own, and give the money to the poor, and you will have treasure in heaven; then come, follow me." When he heard this, he was shocked and went away grieving, for he had many possessions.

(Pause for silent reflection)

Prayer

Lord's Prayer (or alternative)

As the evening shadows come, O God, protect all those dear to my heart, and draw me ever closer to you. Amen.

Week 2
Friday • Morning Prayer

V: I sing as I arise today.
R: I call on my Creator's might:
V: the will of God to be my guide,
R: the eye of God to be my sight,
V: the word of God to be my speech,

R: the hand of God to be my stay,
V: the shield of God to be my strength,
R: the path of God to be my way. Amen.

Psalm 30

I praise you, Yah, because you have saved me
and kept my enemies from gloating over me.
I cried to you for help, my God, and you healed me.
You brought me back from the world of the dead.
I was with those who go down to the depths below,
but you restored my life.
Sing praise to Yah, you faithful people!
Remember what God has done and give thanks!
Yah's anger lasts only a moment,
God's goodness for a lifetime.
There may be tears during the night,
but joy comes in the morning.
I felt secure and said to myself, "I will never be defeated."
You are good to me, Yah,
you have kept me safe as in a mountain fortress.
But when you hid yourself from me, I was filled with fear.
I called to you, Yah; I begged for your help.
What good will come from my death?
What profit from my going to the grave?
Are dead people able to praise you?
Can they proclaim your unfailing goodness?
Help me, Yah, and be merciful! Help me, Yah!
You have changed my sadness into a joyful dance;
you have taken off my clothes of mourning
and given me garments of joy.

So I will not be silent; I will sing praise to you.
Yah, you are my God;
I will give thanks to you forever.

Quote

The road to the sacred leads through the secular.—*Abraham Joshua Heschel*

Amos 5:11–13

Therefore because you trample on the poor and take from them levies of grain, you have built houses of hewn stone, but you shall not live in them; you have planted pleasant vineyards, but you shall not drink their wine. For I know how many are your transgressions, and how great are your sins—you who afflict the righteous, who take a bribe, and push aside the needy in the gate. Therefore the prudent will keep silent in such a time; for it is an evil time.

(Pause for silent reflection)

Prayer

Lord's Prayer (or alternative)

Gracious God, grant me strength, wisdom, and courage to do justice, to love kindness, and to walk humbly with you today.

Week 2
Friday • Evening Prayer

V: O God, lead me to your still waters.
R: Restore my soul.

V: Lead me in right paths.
R: Guide me through the darkest valley.

Psalm 14

Fools say to themselves, "God doesn't matter!"
Such are corrupt; they have done terrible deeds.
There is not one who does what is right.
Yah looks down from heaven
to see if there are any who are wise, any who worship God.
But they have all gone astray; they are all equally bad.
Not one of them does what is right, not a single one.
"Don't they know?" asks Yah.
"Are all these evildoers ignorant? They who eat up my people just
    as they eat bread and do not pray to me?"
But they will become terrified
because God is with those who are just.
They make fun of the plans of the helpless who trust in Yah.
How I pray that salvation will come to Israel from Zion!
When Yah makes the faithful prosperous again,
Jacob and Rachel's descendants will be happy;
the people of Israel will be glad.

Luke 13:10–13

Now [Jesus] was teaching in one of the synagogues on the sabbath. And just then there appeared a woman with a spirit that had crippled her for eighteen years. She was bent over and was quite unable to stand up straight. When Jesus saw her, he called her over and said, "Woman, you are set free from your ailment." When he laid his hands on her, immediately she stood up straight and began praising God.

(Pause for silent reflection)

Prayer

Lord's Prayer (or alternative)

As the evening shadows come, O God, protect all those dear to my heart, and draw me ever closer to you. Amen.

Week 2
Saturday • Morning Prayer

V: Creator of all that is, seen and unseen,
R: Praise to you! Create me anew this day.
V: Savior and Redeemer of the world,
R: Praise to you! Free me from all bondage and oppression.
V: Spirit of life now and eternal,
R: Praise to you! Show me the path I must walk today.

Psalm 112

Alleluia! Happy those who fear Yah
and joyfully keep God's commandments!
Children of such as these will be powers on earth;
each generation of the upright will be blessed.
There will be riches and wealth for their families,
and their righteousness stands firm forever.
Even in the darkness, light dawns for the upright,
for the merciful, compassionate, and righteous.
These good of heart lend graciously,

handling their affairs honestly.
Kept safe by virtue, they are always steadfast
and leave an everlasting memory behind them.
With a trusting heart and confidence in Yah,
they need never fear evil news.
Steadfast in heart, they overcome their fears;
in the end they will triumph over their enemies.
Quick to be generous, they give to the poor;
their righteousness stands firm forever.
People such as these will always be honored.
This fills the wicked with fury
until, grinding their teeth, they waste away,
vanishing like their vain hopes.

Quote

Just as a circle embraces all that is within it, so does the God-head embrace all. No one has the power to divide this circle, to surpass it, or to limit it.—*Hildegard of Bingen*

Isaiah 11:6-9

The wolf shall live with the lamb, the leopard shall lie down with the kid, the calf and the lion and the fatling together, and a little child shall lead them. The cow and the bear shall graze, their young shall lie down together; and the lion shall eat straw like the ox. The nursing child shall play over the hole of the asp, and the weaned child shall put its hand on the adder's den. They will not hurt or destroy on all my holy mountain; for the earth will be full of the knowledge of Yah as the waters cover the sea.

(Pause for silent reflection)

Prayer

Lord's Prayer (or alternative)

Gracious God, grant me strength, wisdom, and courage to do justice, to love kindness, and to walk humbly with you today.

Week 2
Saturday • Evening Prayer

V: O God, lead me to your still waters.
R: Restore my soul.
V: Lead me in right paths.
R: Guide me through the darkest valley.

Psalm 119:33-40

Teach me, O God, the way of your statutes
that I may always observe them.
Give me discernment that I may observe your law
and keep it with all my heart.
Guide me down the path of your commands, for I delight in it.
Turn my heart to your decrees and not to love of gain.
Turn my eyes away from seeing worthless things;
by your way renew my life.
Fulfill your promise to your servant—to those who fear you.
Turn away from me the reproach that I dread,
for your edicts are good.
See, I long for your precepts;
in your justice, give me life.

Luke 16:19–26

There was a rich man who was dressed in purple and fine linen and who feasted sumptuously every day. And at his gate lay a poor man named Lazarus, covered with sores, who longed to satisfy his hunger with what fell from the rich man's table; even the dogs would come and lick his sores. The poor man died and was carried away by the angels to be with Abraham. The rich man also died and was buried. In Hades, where he was being tormented, he looked up and saw Abraham far away with Lazarus by his side. He called out, "Father, Abraham, have mercy on me, and send Lazarus to dip the tip of his finger in water and cool my tongue; for I am in agony in these flames." But Abraham said, "Child, remember that during your lifetime you received your good things, and Lazarus in like manner evil things; but now he is comforted here, and you are in agony. Besides all this, between you and us a great chasm has been fixed, so that those who might want to pass from here to you cannot do so, and no one can cross from there to us."

(Pause for silent reflection)

Prayer

Lord's Prayer (or alternative)

As the evening shadows come, O God, protect all those dear to my heart, and draw me ever closer to you. Amen.

Week 3
Sunday • Morning Prayer

Versicle: God, open my lips.
Response: And my mouth shall proclaim your praise.

Glory be to God our Creator, to Jesus the Christ, and to the Holy Spirit who dwells in our midst, both now and forever. Amen.

Psalm 43

Do me justice, O God,
and plead my cause against a faithless people;
from the deceitful and unjust, rescue me.
For you, O God, are my stronghold.
Why do you keep me so far away?
Why must I go about in mourning, oppressed by the enemy?
Send forth your light and your truth—they shall guide me;
let them bring me to your holy mountain,
to your dwelling place.
Then will I go in to the altar of God,
the God of my delight and joy;
then will I praise you with the harp, O God, my God!
Why are you so downcast, O my soul?
Why do you sigh within me?
Put your hope in God, for I shall again be thankful
in the presence of my savior and my God.

Quote

Hope has two lovely daughters, anger and courage: anger so that what cannot be, may not be; and courage, so that what must be, will be.—*St. Augustine*

Amos 5:21-24

I hate, I despise your festivals, and I take no delight in your solemn assemblies. Even though you offer me your burnt offerings and grain offerings, I will not accept them; and the offerings of well-being of your fatted animals I will not look upon. Take away from me the noise of your songs; I will not listen to the melody of your harps. But let justice roll down like waters, and righteousness like an ever-flowing stream.

(Pause for silent reflection)

Prayer

Lord's Prayer (or alternative)

Merciful God, may my actions and decisions this day be mindful of those who are in need. May justice roll down like waters and righteousness like an ever-flowing stream.

Week 3
Sunday • Evening Prayer

V: Let my prayer rise before you like incense
R: And the lifting up of my hands as an evening sacrifice.
V: Create in me a pure heart, O God,
R: And renew me with a steadfast spirit.

Magnificat

My being proclaims your greatness,
and my spirit finds joy in you, God my Savior.
For you have looked upon me, your servant, in my lowliness;
all ages to come shall call me blessed.
God, you who are mighty have done great things for me.
Holy is your name.
Your mercy is from age to age toward those who fear you.
You have shown might with your arm and confused the proud in their inmost thoughts.
You have deposed the mighty from their thrones
and raised the lowly to high places.
The hungry you have given every good thing
while the rich you have sent away empty.
You have upheld Israel your servant, ever mindful of your mercy even as you promised our ancestors;
promised Abraham, Sarah, and their descendants forever.

Mark 11:15–17

Then they came to Jerusalem. And [Jesus] entered the temple and began to drive out those who were selling and those who were buying in the temple, and he overturned the tables of the money changers and the seats of those who sold doves; and he would not allow anyone to carry anything through the temple. He was teaching and saying, "Is it not written, 'My house shall be called a house of prayer for all the nations'? But you have made it a den of robbers."

(Pause for silent reflection)

Prayer

Lord's Prayer (or alternative)

O God, lift the burdens and cares of this day. Quiet my fears and grant me your peace. Amen.

Week 3
Monday • Morning Prayer

V: O God, come to my assistance.
R: O Christ, make haste to help me.
V: O Sophia, guide my path this day.
R: Blessed Trinity, draw me toward you.

Psalm 19

The heavens proclaim your glory, O God,
and the firmament shows forth the work of your hands.
Day carries the news to day
and night brings the message to night.
No speech, no word, no voice is heard;
yet their news goes forth through all the earth,
their words to the farthest bounds of the world.
There you pitched a tent for the sun;
it comes forth like a bridegroom from his tent,
like a champion eager to run the race.
At the end of the sky is the rising of the sun;
the boundary of the sky is its course.
There is nothing hidden from its scorching heat.
Your law, Yah, is perfect; it refreshes the soul.
Your rule is to be trusted; it gives wisdom to the simple.

Your precepts, Yah, are right; they gladden the heart.
Your command is clear; it gives light to the eyes.
Fear of you, Yah, is holy, abiding forever.
Your decrees are faithful and all of them just.
They are more desirable than gold, than the purest of gold,
and sweeter than honey are they,
than honey oozing from the comb.
So in them your servant finds instruction;
in keeping them is great reward.
But who can detect failings? From hidden faults forgive me.
From presumption restrain your servant,
and let it not rule over me.
Then I shall be blameless, free from grave sin.
May the spoken words of my mouth, the thoughts of my heart,
win favor in your sight, O Yah, my Redeemer, my Rock!

Quote

The geography of faith leads to the cross.—*Daniel Berrigan*

Isaiah 11:1–5

A shoot shall come out from the stump of Jesse, and a branch shall grow out of his roots. The spirit of Yah shall rest on him, the spirit of wisdom and understanding, the spirit of counsel and might, the spirit of knowledge and the fear of Yah. His delight shall be in the fear of Yah. He shall not judge by what his eyes see, or decide by what his ears hear; but with righteousness he shall judge the poor, and decide with equity for the meek of the earth; he shall strike the earth with the rod of his mouth, and with the breath of his lips he shall kill the wicked. Righteousness shall be the belt around his waist, and faithfulness the belt around his loins.

(Pause for silent reflection)

Prayer

Lord's Prayer (or alternative)

Merciful God, may my actions and decisions this day be mindful of those who are in need. May justice roll down like waters and righteousness like an ever-flowing stream.

Week 3
Monday • Evening Prayer

V: Let my prayer rise before you like incense
R: And the lifting up of my hands as an evening sacrifice.
V: Create in me a pure heart, O God,
R: And renew me with a steadfast spirit.

Psalm 121

I lift my eyes to the mountains. Where is help to come from?
My help comes from Yah, who made heaven and earth.
Yah does not let our footsteps slip! Our guard does not sleep.
The guardian of Israel does not slumber or sleep.
Yah guards you, shades you.
With Yah at your right hand the sun cannot harm you by day nor
  the moon at night.
Yah guards you from harm, protects your lives;
Yah watches over your coming and going,
now and for always.

Luke 4:16–21

When [Jesus] came to Nazareth, where he had been brought up, he went to the synagogue on the sabbath day, as was his custom. He stood up to read, and the scroll of the prophet Isaiah was given to him. He unrolled the scroll and found the place where it was written: "The Spirit of Yah is upon me, because Yah has anointed me to bring good news to the poor. Yah has sent me to proclaim release to the captives and recovery of sight to the blind, to let the oppressed go free, to proclaim the year of Yah's favor." And he rolled up the scroll, gave it back to the attendant, and sat down. The eyes of all in the synagogue were fixed on him. Then he began to say to them, "Today this scripture has been fulfilled in your hearing."

(Pause for silent reflection)

Prayer

Lord's Prayer (or alternative)

O God, lift the burdens and cares of this day. Quiet my fears and grant me your peace. Amen.

Week 3
Tuesday • Morning Prayer

V: Weaver of worlds, seen and unseen,
R: Weaver of light and darkness, weal and woe,
V: Weaver of the warp and weft of history,
R: Weave my life into the fabric of your will.

Psalm 57

Have mercy on me, God, have mercy.
In you my soul takes shelter;
I take shelter in the shadow of your wings until the danger passes.
I call out to God the Most High, to God who has blessed me:
to send from heaven and save me,
to rebuke those who trample me.
May God send me faithfulness and love.
I lie down among the lions hungry for human prey;
their teeth are spears and arrows, their tongue like a sharp sword.
Be exalted above the heavens, God.
Let your glory shine on the earth!
They set a snare where I was walking
when I was bowed with care;
they dug a pit for me but fell into it themselves!
My heart is steadfast, God, my heart is steadfast;
I mean to sing and play for you.
Awake, my soul;
awake, lyre and harp.
I mean to wake the dawn!
I mean to thank you among the peoples,
to sing your praise among the nations.
Your love reaches to the heavens,
your faithfulness to the clouds.
Rise high above the heavens, God,
let your glory cover the earth!

Quote

Truth is powerful, and it prevails.—*Sojourner Truth*

Isaiah 40:27–31

Why do you say, O Jacob, and speak, O Israel, "My way is hidden from Yah, and my right is disregarded by my God?" Have you not known? Have you not heard? Yah is the everlasting God, the Creator of the ends of the earth. Yah does not faint or grow weary; Yah's understanding is unsearchable. Yah gives power to the faint and strengthens the powerless. Even youths will faint and be weary, and the young will fall exhausted; but those who wait for Yah shall renew their strength; they shall mount up with wings like eagles, they shall run and not be weary, they shall walk and not faint.

(Pause for silent reflection)

Prayer

Lord's Prayer (or alternative)

Merciful God, may my actions and decisions this day be mindful of those who are in need. May justice roll down like waters and righteousness like an ever-flowing stream.

Week 3
Tuesday • Evening Prayer

V: Let my prayer rise before you like incense
R: And the lifting up of my hands as an evening sacrifice.
V: Create in me a pure heart, O God,
R: And renew me with a steadfast spirit.

Psalm 69:1–13

O God, rescue me! The waters are up to my chin.
I am wallowing in quicksand with no foothold for safety.
I have slipped into deep water; the waves pound over me.
I am exhausted from calling; my throat is parched.
My eyes are strained with looking for my God.
The number of hairs on my head are fewer
than the number of those who hate me without reason.
Wrongful enemies are legion.
How can I restore what I did not steal?
God, you know that I am a fool;
my faults cannot be hidden from you.
Let those who honor you not be ashamed because of me,
O God of hosts.
Let those who seek you not be dismayed because of me,
O God of Israel.
I take insults for your sake, and dishonor covers my face.
I have become an outcast to my ancestors,
a foreigner to my family.
Zeal for your house consumes me.
The insults of blasphemers fall upon me.
By fasting I humbled myself, but this was used to reproach me.

My garment was sackcloth, but I was laughed at by all.
Those who lounge at the city's gate gossip about me,
and I am the subject of drunkards' songs.
As for me, I pray to you for the time of your favor, O God!
In your faithful love and with your constant help, answer me.

John 4:7–14

A Samaritan woman came to draw water, and Jesus said to her, "Give me a drink." (His disciples had gone to the city to buy food.) The Samaritan woman said to him, "How is it that you, a Jew, ask a drink of me, a woman of Samaria?" (Jews do not share things in common with Samaritans.) Jesus answered her, "If you knew the gift of God, and who it is that is saying to you, 'Give me a drink,' you would have asked him, and he would have given you living water." The woman said to him, "Sir, you have no bucket, and the well is deep. Where do you get that living water? Are you greater than our ancestor Jacob, who gave us the well, and with his sons and his flocks drank from it?" Jesus said to her, "Everyone who drinks of this water will be thirsty again, but those who drink of the water that I will give them will never be thirsty. The water that I will give will become in them a spring of water gushing up to eternal life."

(Pause for silent reflection)

Prayer

Lord's Prayer (or alternative)

O God, lift the burdens and cares of this day. Quiet my fears and grant me your peace. Amen.

Week 3
Wednesday • Morning Prayer

V: O Sacred Source of all light,
R: Enlighten my darkness.
V: O God who dwells in uncreated light,
R: In your light, I see light.

Psalm 91

You who dwell in the shelter of the Most High,
who abide in the shadow of the Almighty,
say: "My Refuge and my Strength, my God in whom I trust."
For God will save you from the snare of the fowler,
from the destroying pestilence.
With pinions God will cover you,
and under God's wings you shall find refuge;
God's faithfulness is a guard and a shield.
You will not fear the terror of the night
nor the arrow that flies by day,
nor the pestilence that stalks in darkness,
nor the plague that destroys at noon.
Though a thousand fall at your side,
ten thousand at your ride side, you will remain secure.
Behold, look with your own eyes
and see the punishment of the wicked—
because you have God for your refuge.
You have made the Most High your stronghold.
No harm shall befall you,
nor shall affliction come near your tent;
God has commanded angels to guard you in all your ways.

In their hands they shall raise you up
so that you will not hurt your foot against a stone.
You shall tread upon the lion and the viper;
you shall trample the lion and the dragon.
"Because you cling to me, I will deliver you;
I will protect you because you acknowledge my name.
You shall call upon me, and I will answer you.
I will be with you in times of trouble;
I will deliver you and glorify you
and will show you my salvation."

Quote

The primary confession of the Christian before the world is the deed, which interprets itself . . . the deed alone is our confession of faith before the world.—*Dietrich Bonhoeffer*

Isaiah 1:15–18

When you stretch out your hands, I will hide my eyes from you; even though you make many prayers, I will not listen; your hands are full of blood. Wash yourselves; make yourselves clean; remove the evil of your doings from before my eyes; cease to do evil, learn to do good; seek justice, rescue the oppressed, defend the orphan, plead for the widow. Come now, let us argue it out, says [Yah]: though your sins are like scarlet, they shall be like snow; though they are red like crimson, they shall become like wool.

(Pause for silent reflection)

Prayer

Lord's Prayer (or alternative)

Merciful God, may my actions and decisions this day be mindful of those who are in need. May justice roll down like waters and righteousness like an ever-flowing stream.

Week 3
Wednesday • Evening Prayer

V: Let my prayer rise before you like incense
R: And the lifting up of my hands as an evening sacrifice.
V: Create in me a pure heart, O God,
R: And renew me with a steadfast spirit.

Psalm 28

To you, Yah, I call; my Rock, hear me.
If you do not listen, I shall become like those who are dead.
Hear the voice of my pleading as I cry for help,
as I lift up my hands in prayer to your holy place.
Do not drag me away with the wicked, with the evildoers
who speak words of peace to their neighbors
but have evil in their hearts.
Repay them as their actions merit, for the malice of their deeds.
Repay them for the work of their hands;
give them what they deserve.
For they ignore your deeds, Yah, and the work of your hands.
Blessed be God,
who has heard my cry, my appeal.

You are my strength and my shield.
In you my heart trusts, and I find help;
then my heart rejoices, and I praise you with my song.
You are the strength of your people,
the stronghold where your anointed find salvation.
Save your people; bless Israel, your heritage.
Be their shepherd and carry them forever.

John 5:2-9

Now in Jerusalem by the Sheep Gate there is a pool, called in Hebrew Beth-zatha, which has five porticoes. In these lay many invalids—blind, lame, and paralyzed. One man was there who had been ill for thirty-eight years. When Jesus saw him lying there and knew that he had been there a long time, he said to him, "Do you want to be made well?" The sick man answered him, "Sir, I have no one to put me into the pool when the water is stirred up; and while I am making my way, someone else steps down ahead of me." Jesus said to him, "Stand up, take your mat and walk." At once the man was made well, and he took up his mat and began to walk. Now that day was a sabbath.

(Pause for silent reflection)

Prayer

Lord's Prayer (or alternative)

O God, lift the burdens and cares of this day. Quiet my fears and grant me your peace. Amen.

A SPIRITUALITY FOR DOING JUSTICE

Week 3
Thursday • Morning Prayer

V: All-powerful God,
R: Grant me wisdom to do your will today.
V: All-merciful God,
R: Fill my heart with compassion.
V: All-loving God,
R: Enflame my soul with love of you.

Psalm 146

Alleluia! Praise Yah, O my soul!
I will praise you, Yah, all my life;
I will sing praise to you as long as I live.
Do not put your trust in rulers,
in humans in whom there is no salvation.
When their spirits depart, they return to the earth;
on that very day their plans perish.
Happy those whose help is the God of Jacob and Rachel,
whose hope is in Yah, their God,
the Maker of heaven and earth, the sea, and all that is in them;
who keeps faith forever,
secures justice for the oppressed, and gives food to the hungry.
Yah, you set captives free and give sight to the blind.
You raise up those that were bowed down and love the just.
You protect strangers; the orphan and the widow you sustain,
but the way of the wicked you thwart. Yah shall reign forever—
your God, O Zion, through all generations. Alleluia.

Quote

We are tied together in the single garment of destiny, caught in an inescapable network of mutuality. And whatever affects one directly affects all indirectly. For some strange reason, I can never be what I ought to be until you are what you ought to be. And you can never be what you ought to be until I am what I ought to be. This is the way God's universe is made; this is the way it is structured.—*Martin Luther King Jr.*

Jeremiah 31:31–34

The days are surely coming, says Yah, when I will make a new covenant with the house of Israel and the house of Judah. It will not be like the covenant that I made with their ancestors when I took them out of the land of Egypt—a covenant that they broke, though I was their [spouse], says Yah. But this is the covenant that I will make with the house of Israel after those days, says Yah: I will put my law within them, and I will write it on their hearts; and I will be their God, and they shall be my people. No longer shall they teach one another, or say to each other, "Know Yah," for they shall all know me, from the least of them to the greatest, says Yah; for I will forgive their iniquity and remember their sin no more.

(Pause for silent reflection)

Prayer

Lord's Prayer (or alternative)

Merciful God, may my actions and decisions this day be mindful of those who are in need. May justice roll down like waters and righteousness like an ever-flowing stream.

Week 3
Thursday • Evening Prayer

V: Let my prayer rise before you like incense
R: And the lifting up of my hands as an evening sacrifice.
V: Create in me a pure heart, O God,
R: And renew me with a steadfast spirit.

Psalm 90

Yah, you have been my security
from generation after generation.
Before the mountains were formed or the earth was born,
you are God, without beginning or end.
You turn humans into dust and command: "Go back."
A thousand years are like yesterday to you—come and gone—
no more than a moment in the night.
You sweep humans away like daydreams,
like fresh grass, which springs up and flowers in the morning,
but by evening is withered and dry.
We are consumed by your anger, in terror of your fury.
We stare at our guilt and our secrets
made clear in the light of your face.
All our days pass away in your anger; our lives are over in a sigh.
Seventy years is our life span, or eighty for those who are strong.
These years are painful and empty.
Who comprehends the force of your wrath

and trembles at the strength of your fury?
Make us realize the shortness of our life
that we may gain wisdom of heart.
Yah, relent! Is your anger forever?
Have mercy on your servants.
When morning comes, fill us with your love.
And then we shall celebrate all our days.
Balance our afflictions with joy;
for years we only knew misfortune.
Show your servants what you do for them;
may your glory shine on their children.
May the goodness of [our God] be upon us!
Grant success to the work of our hands.

John 6:47–51

Very truly, I tell you, whoever believes has eternal life. I am the bread of life. Your ancestors ate the manna in the wilderness, and they died. This is the bread that comes down from heaven, so that one may eat of it and not die. I am the living bread that came down from heaven. Whoever eats of this bread will live forever; and the bread that I will give for the life of the world is my flesh.

(Pause for silent reflection)

Prayer

Lord's Prayer (or alternative)

O God, lift the burdens and cares of this day. Quiet my fears and grant me your peace. Amen.

Week 3
Friday • Morning Prayer

V: I sing as I arise today.
R: I call on my Creator's might:
V: the will of God to be my guide,
R: the eye of God to be my sight,
V: the word of God to be my speech,
R: the hand of God to be my stay,
V: the shield of God to be my strength,
R: the path of God to be my way. Amen.

Psalm 116:1-9

I love you, Yah, because you have heard
my voice and my supplications,
because you have inclined your ear to me.
Therefore I will call on you as long as I live.
The cords of death encompassed me;
the pangs of Sheol laid hold on me;
I suffered sorrow and anguish.
Then I called on your name, Yah:
"Oh Yah, I beseech you, save my life!"
Gracious are you, Yah, and righteous;
you are full of compassion.
You protect the simplehearted;
when I was brought low, you saved me.
Be at rest once more, O my soul,
for Yah has been good to you.
For [you] have delivered my soul from death,

my eyes from tears, my feet from stumbling.
I walk before you, Yah, in the land of the living.

Quote

In this life we cannot do great things. We can only do small things with great love.—*Mother Teresa*

Isaiah 10:1–4a

Ah, you who make iniquitous decrees, who write oppressive statutes, to turn aside the needy from justice and to rob the poor of my people of their right, that widows may be your spoil, and that you may make the orphans your prey! What will you do on the day of punishment, in the calamity that will come from far away? To whom will you flee for help, and where will you leave your wealth, so as not to crouch among the prisoners or fall among the slain?

(Pause for silent reflection)

Prayer

Lord's Prayer (or alternative)

Merciful God, may my actions and decisions this day be mindful of those who are in need. May justice roll down like waters and righteousness like an ever-flowing stream.

Week 3
Friday • Evening Prayer

V: Let my prayer rise before you like incense
R: And the lifting up of my hands as an evening sacrifice.
V: Create in me a pure heart, O God,
R: And renew me with a steadfast spirit.

Psalm 46

God is our refuge and our strength,
our ever-present help in distress.
Though the earth trembles, and mountains slide into the sea,
we have no fear.
Waters foam and roar,
and mountains shake at their surging;
but the God of hosts is with us—our stronghold, the God of Israel.
There is a river whose streams give joy to the city of God,
the holy dwelling of the Most High.
God is in its midst; it stands firm.
God will aid it at the break of day.
Even if nations are in chaos, and kingdoms fall,
God's voice resounds; the earth melts away.
[Yah] is with us; the God of Israel is our stronghold.
Come! See the deeds of the Most High,
the marvelous things God has done on earth;
all over the world, God has stopped wars—
breaking bows, splintering spears, burning the shields with fire.
"Be still! and know that I am God,
exalted among the nations, exalted upon the earth."
The Most High is with us;
our stronghold is the God of Israel.

John 11:21-26

Martha said to Jesus, "Lord, if you had been here, my brother would not have died. But even now I know that God will give you whatever you ask . . ." Jesus said to her, "Your brother will rise again." Martha said to him, "I know that he will rise again in the resurrection on the last day." Jesus said to her, "I am the resurrection and the life. Those who believe in me, even though they die, will live, and everyone who lives and believes in me will never die. Do you believe this?"

(Pause for silent reflection)

Prayer

Lord's Prayer (or alternative)

O God, lift the burdens and cares of this day. Quiet my fears and grant me your peace. Amen.

Week 3
Saturday • Morning Prayer

V: Creator of all that is, seen and unseen,
R: Praise to you! Create me anew this day.
V: Savior and Redeemer of the world,
R: Praise to you! Free me from all bondage and oppression.
V: Spirit of life, now and eternal,
R: Praise to you! Show me the path I must walk today.

Psalm 32

Happy are those whose fault is taken away, whose sin is covered.
Happy those whose sin Yah does not count,
in whose spirit there is no guile.
As long as I would not speak,
my bones wasted away with groaning all day long;
for day and night, your hand lay heavy upon me.
My strength was dried up as by the summer's heat.
Then I acknowledged my sin to you and did not cover my guilt.
I said, "I confess my faults to you,"
and you took away the guilt of my sin.
For this shall all the faithful pray to you in time of stress.
Though deep waters rise, they shall not reach them.
You are my shelter; you will protect me from trouble
and surround me with songs of deliverance.
I will instruct you and show you the way you should walk;
I will counsel you and watch over you.
Do not be senseless like horses or mules,
their tempers curbed only by bridle and bit,
or they will not come near you.
Many are the sorrows of the wicked,
but faithful love surrounds those who trust in you.
Rejoice and be glad in [Yah], you just;
exult, all you upright of heart.

Quote

There is something in every one of you that wants and listens for the sound of the genius in yourself. It is the only true guide you will ever have. And if you cannot hear it, you will all of your life

spend your days on the ends of strings that somebody else pulls.
—*Howard Thurman*

Micah 6:6–8

"With what shall I come before Yah, and bow myself before God on high? Shall I come before [God] with burnt offerings, with calves a year old? Will Yah be pleased with thousands of rams, with ten thousands of rivers of oil? Shall I give my firstborn for my transgression, the fruit of my body for the sin of my soul?" [God] has told you, O mortal, what is good; and what does Yah require of you but to do justice, and to love kindness, and to walk humbly with your God?

(Pause for silent reflection)

Prayer

Lord's Prayer (or alternative)

Merciful God, may my actions and decisions this day be mindful of those who are in need. May justice roll down like waters and righteousness like an ever-flowing stream.

Week 3
Saturday • Evening Prayer

V: Let my prayer rise before you like incense
R: And the lifting up of my hands as an evening sacrifice.
V: Create in me a pure heart, O God,
R: And renew me with a steadfast spirit.

A SPIRITUALITY FOR DOING JUSTICE

Psalm 55:1–11, 20–23

Hear my prayer, O God; do not hide yourself from my petition.
Listen to me and answer me.
In restlessness I groan and am troubled
because of the voice of the enemy,
because of the threats of the wicked.
For they engulf me with their mischief,
and in anger they assault me.
My heart is distressed within me,
and terrors of death come down on me.
Fear and trembling get hold of me, and horror overwhelms me.
So I said, "Oh, had I the wings of a dove!
Then I would fly away and be at rest.
Yes, then I would flee far away and lodge in the desert.
I would hasten to my place of refuge
from this raging wind and storm."
Destroy them, my Refuge, confuse their speech,
for I have seen violence and strife in the city.
Day and night they go about on the walls;
evil and trouble are in its center.
Violence is within the city, and from the marketplace oppression
and fraud are never absent.
Each one lays hands on allies and violates their pact.
Their mouths are smoother than butter,
but in their hearts there is war;
their words are softer than oil,
yet they are drawn swords.
Cast your cares on God, who will sustain you
and will never allow the righteous to fall.
But you, O God, will bring down the wicked

into the pit of destruction;
the deceitful shall not live out half their days.
I will trust in you.

John 15:12–14

This is my commandment, that you love one another as I have loved you. No one has greater love than this, to lay down one's life for one's friends. You are my friends if you do what I command you.

(Pause for silent reflection)

Prayer

Lord's Prayer (or alternative)

O God, lift the burdens and cares of this day. Quiet my fears and grant me your peace. Amen.

Week 4
Sunday • Morning Prayer

Versicle: God, open my lips.
Response: And my mouth shall proclaim your praise.

Glory be to God our Creator, to Jesus the Christ, and to the Holy Spirit who dwells in our midst, both now and forever. Amen.

Psalm 5

Harken to my words, O God, attend to my musing.
Heed my call for help; to you I pray.
In the morning you hear my voice;
at dawn I will make ready and watch for you.
For you, O God, delight not in wickedness;
no one who is evil remains with you.
The arrogant may not stand in your sight;
you hate all who do futile things.
You destroy all who speak falsehood;
the bloodthirsty and the deceitful you detest.
But I, through your abundant kindness, will enter your house;
I will worship at your holy Temple in fear of you.
Because of my enemies, guide me in your justice;
make straight your way before me.
For in their mouths there is no truth;

their hearts teem with treacheries.
Their throats are open graves; they flatter with their tongues.
Hold them guilty, O God;
let them fall by their own devices.
For their many sins, cast them out,
for they have rebelled against you.
But let all who take refuge in you be glad and rejoice forever.
Protect them, O God, bless the just;
surround them like a shield and crown them with your favor.

Quote

The bread that you store up belongs to the hungry; the coat that lies in your chest belongs to the naked; the gold that you have hidden in the ground belongs to the poor.—*St. Basil of Caesarea*

Jeremiah 7:1–11

The word that came to Jeremiah from Yah: Stand in the gate of Yah's house, and proclaim there this word, and say, Hear the word of Yah, all you people of Judah, you that enter these gates to worship Yah. Thus says Yah Sabaoth, the God of Israel: Amend your ways and your doings, and let me dwell with you in this place. Do not trust in these deceptive words: "This is the temple of Yah, the temple of Yah, the temple of Yah." For if you truly amend your ways and your doings, if you truly act justly with one another, if you do not oppress the alien, the orphan, and the widow, or shed innocent blood in this place, and if you do not go after other gods to your own hurt, then I will dwell with you in this place, in the land that I gave of old to your ancestors forever and ever. Here you are, trusting in deceptive words to no avail. Will you steal, murder, commit adultery, swear falsely, make offerings to Baal, and go after other gods that you have not known, and then come and stand before me in this house, which is called by my name, and say, "We are safe!"—only to go on doing all these abominations? Has this house, which is called by my name, become a den of robbers in your sight? You know, I too am watching, says Yah.

(Pause for silent reflection)

Prayer

Lord's Prayer (or alternative)

Make known to me the path that I must walk this day, O God, and help me to walk it. Deepen me in faithful service to those in need, open my eyes to the wonder of your creation, bless those dear to my heart, and grant me joy in living. Amen.

Week 4
Sunday • Evening Prayer

V: God, you are my light and my salvation.
R: In your presence, my fears subside.
V: You have said, "Seek my face."
R: Your face, O God, I do seek.
V: Hide not your face from your servant.
R: Show me your light and your salvation.

Magnificat

My being proclaims your greatness,
and my spirit finds joy in you, God my Savior.

For you have looked upon me, your servant, in my lowliness;
all ages to come shall call me blessed.

God, you who are mighty have done great things for me.
Holy is your name.
Your mercy is from age to age toward those who fear you.
You have shown might with your arm and confused the proud in their inmost thoughts.
You have deposed the mighty from their thrones
and raised the lowly to high places.
The hungry you have given every good thing
while the rich you have sent away empty.
You have upheld Israel your servant, ever mindful of your mercy even as you promised our ancestors;
promised Abraham, Sarah, and their descendants forever.

John 12:24–26a

"Very truly, I tell you, unless a grain of wheat falls into the earth and dies, it remains just a single grain; but if it dies, it bears much fruit. Those who love their life lose it, and those who hate their life in this world will keep it for eternal life. Whoever serves me must follow me, and where I am, there will my servant be also."

(Pause for silent reflection)

Prayer

Lord's Prayer (or alternative)

Renew me, O God. Grant me power in my weariness, wisdom in my uncertainty, and peace in the restlessness of my soul.

Week 4
Monday • Morning Prayer

V: O God, come to my assistance.
R: O Christ, make haste to help me.
V: O Sophia, guide my path this day.
R: Blessed Trinity, draw me toward you.

Psalm 25:1–13

To you, Yah, I lift up my soul. O my God, in you I trust.
Let me not be put to shame;
let not my enemies exult over me.
Let none that wait for you be put to shame;
let them be ashamed who heedlessly break faith.
Make me know your ways, Yah; teach me your paths.
Lead me in your truth and teach me,
for you are the God of my salvation; for you I wait all the day long.
Be mindful of your mercy, Yah,
and of your steadfast love, for they have been from of old.
Remember not the sins of my youth, or my transgressions;
according to your steadfast love remember me,
because of your goodness, Yah!
Good and upright is Yah, instructing sinners in the way,
leading the humble in what is right,
and teaching the poor the way.
All the paths of Yah are steadfast love and faithfulness
for those who keep God's covenant and decrees.
For your name's sake, O Yah, pardon my guilt, for it is great.
Who are they who fear you?
Those you instruct in the way that they should choose.

They shall abide in prosperity,
and their children shall possess the land.

Quote

The most potent weapon in the hands of the oppressor is the mind of the oppressed.—*Stephen Biko*

Isaiah 43:1-3a

But now thus says Yah, who created you, O Jacob, who formed you, O Israel: Do not fear, for I have redeemed you; I have called you by name, you are mine. When you pass through the waters, I will be with you; and through the rivers, they shall not overwhelm you; when you walk through fire, you shall not be burned, and the flame shall not consume you. For I am Yah your God, the Holy One of Israel, your Savior.

(Pause for silent reflection)

Prayer

Lord's Prayer (or alternative)

Make known to me the path that I must walk this day, O God, and help me to walk it. Deepen me in faithful service to those in need, open my eyes to the wonder of your creation, bless those dear to my heart, and grant me joy in living.

Week 4
Monday • Evening Prayer

V: God, you are my light and my salvation.
R: In your presence, my fears subside.
V: You have said, "Seek my face."
R: Your face, O God, I do seek.
V: Hide not your face from your servant.
R: Show me your light and your salvation.

Psalm 37:1–11

Fret not because of the wicked; be not envious of wrongdoers!
For they will soon fade like the grass
and wither like the green herb.
Trust in Yah and do good
so you will dwell in the land and enjoy security.
Take delight in Yah,
who will give you the desires of your heart.
Commit your way to Yah; trust in God, who will act,
bringing forth your vindication as the light
and your right as the noonday sun.
Be still before Yah and wait patiently;
fret not over those who prosper, over those who carry out evil.
Refrain from anger and forsake wrath!
Fret not; it tends only to evil.
For the wicked shall be cut off,
but those who wait for Yah shall possess the land.
Yet a little while and the wicked will be no more;
though you look well at their place, they will not be there.
But the meek shall possess the land
and delight themselves in abundance.

John 8:31-32

Then Jesus said to [those] who had believed in him, "If you continue in my word, you are truly my disciples; and you will know the truth, and the truth will make you free."

(Pause for silent reflection)

Prayer

Lord's Prayer (or alternative)

Renew me, O God. Grant me power in my weariness, wisdom in my uncertainty, and peace in the restlessness of my soul.

Week 4
Tuesday • Morning Prayer

V: Weaver of worlds, seen and unseen,
R: Weaver of light and darkness, weal and woe,
V: Weaver of the warp and weft of history,
R: Weave my life into the fabric of your will.

Psalm 115:1-9

Not to us, Yah, not to us, but to you alone give the glory
because of your love and your faithfulness.
Or some nations will say: "Where is their God?"
But our God is in the heavens doing whatever God wills.
Their idols are silver and gold, the work of human hands.
They have mouths but cannot speak;

they have eyes but cannot see;
they have ears but cannot hear;
they have nostrils but cannot smell.
With their hands they cannot feel;
with their feet they cannot walk.
No sound comes from their throats.
Those who make them will be like them,
and so will all who trust in them.
Descendants of Israel, trust in Yah,
who is your help and your shield.

Quote

We have all known the long loneliness, and we have learned that the only solution is love and that love comes with community.
—*Dorothy Day*

Habakkuk 2:1–3

I will stand at my watchpost, and station myself on the rampart; I will keep watch to see what God will say to me, and what God will answer concerning my complaint. Then Yah answered me and said: Write the vision; make it plain on tablets, so that a runner may read it. For there is still a vision for the appointed time; it speaks of the end, and does not lie. If it seems to tarry, wait for it; it will surely come, it will not delay.

(Pause for silent reflection)

Prayer

Lord's Prayer (or alternative)

Make known to me the path that I must walk this day, O God, and help me to walk it. Deepen me in faithful service to those in need, open my eyes to the wonder of your creation, bless those dear to my heart, and grant me joy in living. Amen.

Week 4
Tuesday • Evening Prayer

V: God, you are my light and my salvation.
R: In your presence, my fears subside.
V: You have said, "Seek my face."
R: Your face, O God, I do seek.
V: Hide not your face from your servant.
R: Show me your light and your salvation.

Psalm 4

Answer me when I call, God, my defender!
When I was in trouble, you came to my help.
Be kind to me now; hear my prayer!
How long will you people insult me?
How long will you love what is worthless and seek what is false?
Remember that Yah has chosen me and hears me when I call.
Tremble, and stop your sinning;
think deeply about this, alone and silent in your rooms.
Offer the right sacrifices to the Holy One
and put your trust in God.

There are many who say, "How we wish to receive a blessing!"
Look on us with kindness, Yah!
The joy that you give me is much greater
than the joy of those who have an abundance of grain and wine.
As soon as I lie down, I peacefully go to sleep;
you alone, my Strength, keep me perfectly safe.

Matthew 25:31–40

When the Son of Man comes in his glory, and all the angels with him, then he will sit on the throne of his glory. All the nations will be gathered before him, and he will separate people from one another as a shepherd separates the sheep from the goats, and he will put the sheep at his right hand and the goats at his left. Then the king will say to those at his right hand, "Come, you that are blessed by my Father, inherit the kingdom prepared for you from the foundation of the world; for I was hungry and you gave me food, I was thirsty and you gave me something to drink, I was a stranger and you welcomed me, I was naked and you gave me clothing, I was sick and you took care of me, I was in prison and you visited me." Then the righteous will answer him, "Lord, when was it that we saw you hungry and gave you food, or thirsty and gave you something to drink? And when was it that we saw you a stranger and welcomed you, or naked and gave you clothing? And when was it that we saw you sick or in prison and visited you?" And the king will answer them, "Truly I tell you, just as you did it to one of the least of these who are members of my family, you did it to me."

(Pause for silent reflection)

Prayer

Lord's Prayer (or alternative)

Renew me, O God. Grant me power in my weariness, wisdom in my uncertainty, and peace in the restlessness of my soul.

Week 4
Wednesday • Morning Prayer

V: O Sacred Source of all light,
R: Enlighten my darkness.
V: O God who dwells in uncreated light,
R: In your light, I see light.

Psalm 44:1-3, 19-26

O God, we have heard with our ears,
our ancestors have told us all the deeds that you did in their days,
all the work of your hand in days long ago.
You planted them in the land and drove the nations out;
you made them strike root, scattering the other peoples.
It was not our ancestors' swords that won them the land, nor their
    arm that gave them the victory—
but your right hand and your arm and the light of your face.
Such was your favor to them.
Yet you crushed us as the sea serpent was crushed
and covered us with darkness.
If we had forgotten the name of our God
and spread our hands in prayer to any other,
would not God find this out—

for God knows the secrets of the heart.
Because of you we face death all day long
and are considered as sheep for slaughter.
Rouse yourself—why do you sleep?
Awake, do not reject us forever.
Why do you hide your face,
forgetting our misery and our sufferings?
For we sink down to the dust and cling to the ground.
Rise up and come to our help;
because of your unfailing love, set us free.

Quote

Darkness cannot drive out darkness; only light can do that. Hate cannot drive out hate; only love can do that.—*Martin Luther King Jr.*

Proverbs 28:3-6

A ruler who oppresses the poor is a beating rain that leaves no food. Those who forsake the law praise the wicked, but those who keep the law struggle against them. The evil do not understand justice, but those who seek Yah understand it completely. Better to be poor and walk in integrity than to be crooked in one's ways even though rich.

(Pause for silent reflection)

Prayer

Lord's Prayer (or alternative)

Make known to me the path that I must walk this day, O God, and help me to walk it. Deepen me in faithful service to those in need, open my eyes to the wonder of your creation, bless those dear to my heart, and grant me joy in living.

Week 4
Wednesday • Evening Prayer

V: God, you are my light and my salvation.
R: In your presence, my fears subside.
V: You have said, "Seek my face."
R: Your face, O God, I do seek.
V: Hide not your face from your servant.
R: Show me your light and your salvation.

Psalm 73:1-12, 22-28

God is indeed good to Israel, to the pure in heart.
But my feet were almost stumbling;
my steps had nearly slipped,
because I was jealous of the boasters
and begrudged the wealth of the wicked.
There is no such thing as pain for them;
their bodies are healthy and strong.
They do not suffer as others do; no human misery for them!
So pride is their chain of honor,

violence the robe that adorns them.
Their malice oozes like grease;
their hearts overflow with schemes.
They scoff and speak evil;
arrogantly they talk of oppression.
They think their mouth is heaven
and their tongue can dictate on earth.
This is why my people turn to them and sip up all they say,
asking, "How will God find out?
Does the Most High know everything?
Look at them: these are the wicked,
well-off and still they increase in riches."
I had been foolish and misunderstood;
I was like a stupid beast before you.
Nevertheless, I waited in your presence;
you grasped my right hand.
Now guide me with your counsel
and receive me into glory at last.
No one else in heaven can attract me;
I delight in nothing else on earth.
My flesh and my heart ache with love,
my heart's foundation, my own, God forever!
Truly, to abandon you is to perish.
You destroy everyone who is unfaithful;
as for me, my joy lies in being close to God.
I have taken shelter in you,
continually to proclaim what you have done.

Matthew 19:23-26

Then Jesus said to his disciples, "Truly I tell you, it will be hard for a rich person to enter the kingdom of heaven. Again I tell you, it is easier for a camel to go through the eye of a needle than for someone who is rich to enter the kingdom of God." When the disciples heard this, they were greatly astounded and said, "Then who can be saved?" But Jesus looked at them and said, "For mortals it is impossible, but for God all things are possible."

(Pause for silent reflection)

Prayer

Lord's Prayer (or alternative)

Renew me, O God. Grant me power in my weariness, wisdom in my uncertainty, and peace in the restlessness of my soul.

Week 4
Thursday • Morning Prayer

V: All-powerful God,
R: Grant me wisdom to do your will today.
V: All-merciful God,
R: Fill my heart with compassion.
V: All-loving God,
R: Enflame my soul with love of you.

Psalm 67

God, show your faithfulness, bless us,
and make your face smile on us!
For then the earth will acknowledge your ways,
and all the nations will know of your power to save.
May all the nations praise you, O God;
may all the nations praise you!
Let the nations shout and sing for joy
since you dispense true justice to the world.
You grant strict justice to the peoples;
on earth you guide the nations.
Let the nations praise you, God;
let all the nations praise you!
The soil has given its harvest;
God, our God, has blessed us.
May God continue to bless us;
and let God be feared to the very ends of the earth.

Quote

When I feed the poor, they call me a saint; when I ask why they are poor, they call me a communist.—*Archbishop Dom Helder Camara*

Malachi 3:1b–2, 5

The messenger of the covenant in whom you delight—indeed, he is coming, says Yah Sabaoth. But who can endure the day of his coming, and who can stand when he appears? For he is like a refiner's fire and like fullers' soap. . . . Then I will draw near to you for judgment; I will be swift to bear witness against the sorcerers, against the adulterers, against those who swear falsely, against those who oppress the hired workers in their wages, the widow and the orphan, against those who thrust aside the alien, and do not fear me, says Yah Sabaoth.

(Pause for silent reflection)

Prayer

Lord's Prayer (or alternative)

Make known to me the path that I must walk this day, O God, and help me to walk it. Deepen me in faithful service to those in need, open my eyes to the wonder of your creation, bless those dear to my heart, and grant me joy in living.

Week 4
Thursday • Evening Prayer

V: God, you are my light and my salvation.
R: In your presence, my fears subside.
V: You have said, "Seek my face."
R: Your face, O God, I do seek.
V: Hide not your face from your servant.
R: Show me your light and your salvation.

Psalm 49:1–15

Hear this! Listen, all people everywhere,
both great and small alike, rich and poor together.
My heart is full of insight; I will speak words of wisdom.

I will turn my attention to a proverb
and unravel its meaning as I play the harp.
I am not afraid in times of danger,
when I am surrounded by wicked enemies—
those who trust in their riches and boast of their great wealth.
People can never redeem themselves,
cannot pay God the price for their ransom,
because the payment for their life is too great.
What they can pay will never be enough
to keep them from destruction, to let them live forever.
They see that even the wise die,
as well as the foolish and senseless.
They all leave their riches to others.
Their tombs are their homes forever; there they stay for all time,
even though they once had lands of their own.
Their greatness cannot keep them from death;
they will die like the animals.
See what happens to those who trust in themselves—
the fate of those who are satisfied with their wealth:
they are doomed to die like sheep, and death is their shepherd. The
righteous will rule over them in the morning
as their bodies decay in the land of the dead,
far from their homes!
But God will redeem me
and will take me from the power of death.

Matthew 6:25-34

Therefore I tell you, do not worry about your life, what you will eat or what you will drink, or about your body, what you will wear. Is not life more than food, and the body more than clothing? Look at the birds of the air; they neither sow nor reap nor gather into barns, and yet your heavenly Father feeds them. Are you not of more value than they? And can any of you by worrying add a single hour to your span of life? And why do you worry about clothing? Consider the lilies of the field, how they grow: they neither toil nor spin, yet I tell you, even Solomon in all his glory was not clothed like one of these. But if God so clothes the grass of the field, which is alive today and tomorrow is thrown into the oven, will God not much more clothe you—you of little faith? Therefore do not worry, saying, "What will we eat?" or "What will we drink?" or "What will we wear?" For it is the Gentiles who strive for all these things; and indeed your heavenly Father knows that you need all these things. But strive first for the kingdom of God and [its] righteousness, and all these things will be given to you as well. So do not worry about tomorrow, for tomorrow will bring worries of its own. Today's trouble is enough for today.

(Pause for silent reflection)

Prayer

Lord's Prayer (or alternative)

Renew me, O God. Grant me power in my weariness, wisdom in my uncertainty, and peace in the restlessness of my soul.

Week 4
Friday • Morning Prayer

V: I sing as I arise today.
R: I call on my Creator's might:
V: the will of God to be my guide,

R: the eye of God to be my sight,
V: the word of God to be my speech,
R: the hand of God to be my stay,
V: the shield of God to be my strength,
R: the path of God to be my way. Amen.

Psalm 103:1–13

Bless Yah, O my soul.
Bless God's holy name, all that is in me!
Bless Yah, O my soul, and remember God's faithfulness:
in forgiving all your offenses, in healing all your diseases,
in redeeming your life from destruction,
in crowning you with love and compassion,
in filling your years with good things,
in renewing your youth like an eagle's.
Yah does justice and always takes the side of the oppressed.
God's ways were revealed to Moses,
and Yah's deeds to Israel.
Yah is merciful and forgiving, slow to anger, rich in love;
Yah's wrath does not last forever; it exists a short time only.
We are never threatened, never punished
as our guilt and our sins deserve.
As the height of heaven over earth
is the greatness of Yah's faithful love for those who fear God.
Yah takes our sins away farther than the east is from the west.
As tenderly as parents treat their children,
so Yah has compassion on those who fear God.

Quote

Faith is taking the first step even when you don't see the whole staircase.—*Martin Luther King Jr.*

Joel 2:28-29

Then afterward I will pour out my spirit on all flesh; your sons and your daughters shall prophesy, your old men shall dream dreams, and your young men shall see visions. Even on the male and female slaves, in those days, I will pour out my spirit.

(Pause for silent reflection)

Prayer

Lord's Prayer (or alternative)

Make known to me the path that I must walk this day, O God, and help me to walk it. Deepen me in faithful service to those in need, open my eyes to the wonder of your creation, bless those dear to my heart, and grant me joy in living.

Week 4
Friday • Evening Prayer

V: God, you are my light and my salvation.
R: In your presence, my fears subside.
V: You have said, "Seek my face."
R: Your face, O God, I do seek.
V: Hide not your face from your servant.
R: Show me your light and your salvation.

Psalm 6

Yah, rebuke me not in your anger,
nor chasten me in your wrath.
Be gracious to me, for I am weak;
heal me, for my heart is troubled.
My soul also is sorely troubled.
Turn and save my life;
deliver me for the sake of your steadfast love,
for in death you are not remembered.
In Sheol who can sing your praise?
I am weary with my moaning;
every night I flood my bed with tears,
I drench my couch with my weeping.
My eyes waste away because of grief;
I grow weak because of my foes.
Leave me, all you worshippers of idols,
for Yah has heard the sound of my weeping.
Yah has heard my supplication and accepts my prayer.
All my enemies shall be ashamed and greatly troubled;
they shall turn back and be put to shame in a moment.

John 14:26–27

But the Advocate, the Holy Spirit, whom the Father will send in my name, will teach you everything, and remind you of all that I have said to you. Peace I leave with you; my peace I give to you. I do not give to you as the world gives. Do not let your hearts be troubled, and do not let them be afraid.

(Pause for silent reflection)

Prayer

Lord's Prayer (or alternative)

Renew me, O God. Grant me power in my weariness, wisdom in my uncertainty, and peace in the restlessness of my soul.

Week 4
Saturday • Morning Prayer

V: Creator of all that is, seen and unseen,
R: Praise to you! Create me anew this day.
V: Savior and Redeemer of the world,
R: Praise to you! Free me from all bondage and oppression.
V: Spirit of life now and eternal,
R: Praise to you! Show me the path I must walk today.

Psalm 33:1–11

Sing out your joy to the Creator, good people;
for praise is fitting for loyal hearts.
Give thanks to the Creator upon the harp,
with a ten-stringed lute sing songs.
O sing a new song; play skillfully and loudly so that all may hear.
For the word of the Creator is faithful,
and all God's works are to be trusted.
The Creator loves justice and right
and fills the earth with faithful love.
By the Creator's word the heavens were made,
by the breath of God's mouth all the stars.
The Creator collects the waves of the ocean

and gathers up the depths of the sea.
Let all the earth fear the Creator,
all who live in the world honor God.
The Creator spoke, and it came to be;
commanded, it sprang into existence.
The Creator frustrates the plans of the nations,
overthrows the designs of the peoples.
The Creator's own designs shall last forever,
the plans of God's heart for all ages.

Quote

All shall be well, and all shall be well, and all manner of things shall be well.—*Julian of Norwich*

Isaiah 40:1–5

Comfort, O comfort my people, says your God. Speak tenderly to Jerusalem, and cry to her that she has served her term, that her penalty is paid, that she has received from Yah's hand double for all her sins. A voice cries out: "In the wilderness prepare the way of Yah, make straight in the desert a highway for our God. Every valley shall be lifted up, and every mountain and hill be made low; the uneven ground shall become level, and the rough places a plain. Then the glory of Yah shall be revealed, and all people shall see it together, for the mouth of Yah has spoken."

(Pause for silent reflection)

Prayer

Lord's Prayer (or alternative)

Make known to me the path that I must walk this day, O God, and help me to walk it. Deepen me in faithful service to those in need, open my eyes to the wonder of your creation, bless those dear to my heart, and grant me joy in living.

Week 4
Saturday • Evening Prayer

V: God, you are my light and my salvation.
R: In your presence, my fears subside.
V: You have said, "Seek my face."
R: Your face, O God, I do seek.
V: Hide not your face from your servant.
R: Show me your light and your salvation.

Psalm 111

Alleluia! I will thank you, Yah, with all my heart
in the meeting of the just and their assembly.
Great are your works to be pondered by all who love them.
Glorious and sublime are your works;
your justice stands firm forever.
You help us remember your wonders.
You are compassion and love.
You have given food to those who fear you,
keeping your covenant ever in mind.
You have shown your might to your people
by giving them the lands of the nations.

Your works are justice and truth;
your precepts are all of them sure;
they are steadfast forever and ever,
made in uprightness and faithfulness.
You have sent deliverance to your people
and established your covenant forever.
Holy your name, greatly to be feared.
To fear you is the beginning of wisdom;
all who do so prove themselves wise.
Your praise shall last forever!

John 17:11, 15–18

And now I am no longer in the world, but they are in the world, and I am coming to you. Holy Father, protect them in your name that you have given me, so that they may be one, as we are one. I am not asking you to take them out of the world, but I ask you to protect them from the evil one. They do not belong to the world, just as I do not belong to the world. Sanctify them in the truth; your word is truth. As you have sent me into the world, so I have sent them into the world.

(Pause for silent reflection)

Prayer

Lord's Prayer (or alternative)

Renew me, O God. Grant me power in my weariness, wisdom in my uncertainty, and peace in the restlessness of my soul.

Gallery of Icons

GALLERY OF ICONS

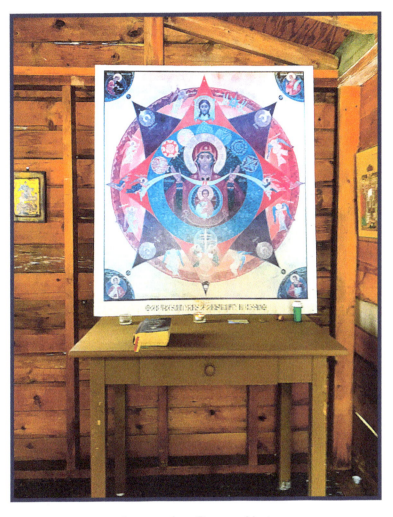

Image A   Prayer Hut

Image B *Elijah in the Cave*

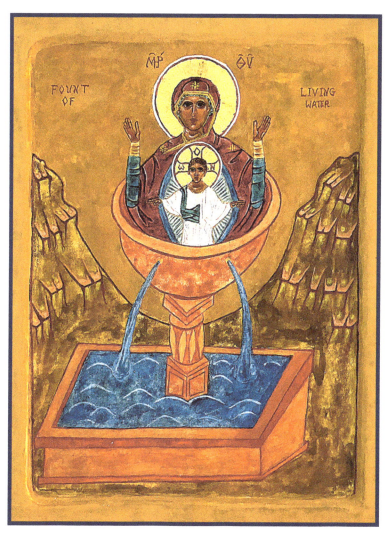

Image C   *Fount of Living Water*

Image D *Hagia Sophia*

Image E *Acheiropoietos*

Image F   *Archangel Michael*

Image G *St. Francis and the Sultan*

Image H   *St. George and the Dragon*

Image 1 *Dorothy Day*

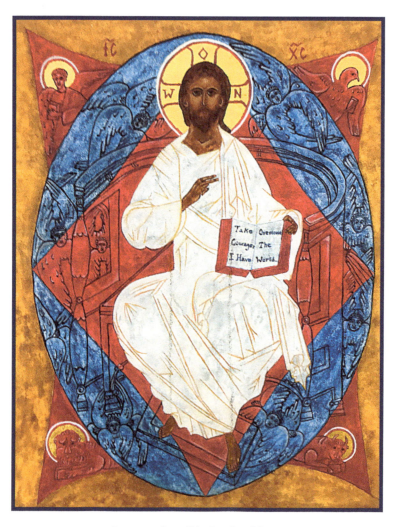

Image J   *Christ in Glory*